SUPREME
ARROGANCE

How the
SUPREME COURT IGNORED
THE CONSTITUTION
AND WRECKED AMERICA

BY

Chris Marrou

ISBN: 0615656099
ISBN 13: 9780615656090

Library of Congress Control Number: 2012910739
CreateSpace, North Charleston, SC

CONTENTS

WHOSE CONSTITUTION IS IT?

In early 2011 *The New Yorker* published an article titled "The Cult of the Constitution," by Jill Lepore. It was a typical liberal screed—Ms. Lepore is a history professor at Harvard University. In it she managed to avoid saying much of anything about the liberal view of the Constitution—which is generally, "The Constitution is what we say it is whenever we have enough votes to win a Supreme Court decision"—while dropping bombs on the originist view that the Constitution meant something when it was written and approved and still means something today. Despite the title of the piece, her complaints were typical and mild, the quiet murmur that liberals have when speaking to each other at a sustainable, fair-trade, zero-emissions coffee shop: the Second Amendment didn't mean everyone could own a gun, but only that citizens could form militias; most people have never read the Constitution, and even more of them aren't sure what is in it; the Constitution once allowed people to own slaves, which for liberals is enough of a condemnation to justify throwing out the entire document.

But the title of Dr. Lepore's article did make me realize something about the issue of the Constitution in America today. I believe the great divide over the Constitution is based on an untruth liberals must believe in order to achieve their goals in this country. Liberals, of course, think their view of the world is the correct one, with its Eurocentric, nanny-state restrictions disguised as help and freedom for every personal desire except when those desires involve business or the environment. The only problem is that when such views are stated openly, the American public almost never votes to approve them. Gay marriage, which Dr. Lepore referred to in her article, is a particular favorite of the left, but it has never been approved in a referendum over its legality. So rather than accept defeat, liberals turned to the courts and found liberal judges who would simply say that it was unconstitutional *not* to allow gay marriage.

And this is where the true misunderstanding of the Constitution lies. Liberals who claim conservatives have made a cult of the Constitution are themselves quite the cultists of the document—or their view of the document. Their cult demands the belief that the Constitution contains whatever laws they want applied to the entire United States. And why not? If everything that controls this nation is in the Constitution, their lives are much easier; the ACLU and its ilk need only go to federal courts and find sympathetic federal judges who will decide that the Constitution contains whatever they want at that particular moment, avoiding such inconvenient things as state legislatures, the public, and elections.

The truth is that the Constitution was never meant to contain everything necessary to run this country, even when it was only thirteen states with four million people. The Constitution is simply a template for how the federal government should be set up, with very few rules for what the individual states can and cannot do. Note the issue of slavery, which liberals love to bring up to throw mud on the Constitution. Believing that all thirteen colonies were needed if the United States were to win its independence, the Constitution finessed the issue of slavery by barely mentioning it, stating that importation of slaves had to end by 1808 and that slaves would be counted as three-fifths of a person for the allocation of congressional districts.[1] If the Constitution were all that mattered in the law of this nation, slavery could have been extended to every state in the union until the Thirteenth, Fourteenth, and Fifteenth Amendments were passed, banning the practice. But it wasn't. Using the gay-marriage logic, a federal judge in the early nineteenth century could have found that it was unconstitutional *not* to allow slavery in every state because it was allowed in some states and therefore "constitutional," just as some judges today claim that

---

[1] That issue led to one of the greatest misunderstandings of the Constitutional Convention. Many people believe this was how white people viewed and valued blacks in that day: as less than a whole human. In fact, it was the *slave* states that wanted slaves fully counted so they could have more congressional seats and expand the practice of slavery. Northern interests who opposed slavery came up with the three-fifths rule so Congress would include more antislavery seats in hopes of ending the practice. But, hey, don't confuse yourself with the facts.

since it's legal for men and women to marry in all states, it must be legal for men and men to marry, and anything less is a curtailment of constitutional rights.

Likewise, a federal judge in the 1800s could have ruled that women were not allowed to vote in this country until the Nineteenth Amendment was passed in 1920, but in fact women were allowed to vote in a number of states before that time. Wyoming granted women the right to vote in 1869 when it was a territory and brought that right along when it became a state in 1890; Utah allowed women the right to vote when it was a territory in 1870, even though it still allowed polygamy and brought that right into the union in 1890, although polygamy was disallowed. (The Constitution, it must be added, never said anything about polygamy, either.)

Sigmund Freud developed the psychological concept of projection: the practice of seeing one's own defects in others to avoid seeing them in oneself. That's how it is with the Constitution. Despite the way the issue has been presented in the media, it's conservatives who *don't* need everything to be in the Constitution; liberals, on the other hand, *must* find everything there because the other means of achieving their political desires—elections—are often so unsuccessful for them. And even though there have been many changes in recent years, this nation remains conservative at its core.

Liberals who need to have the Constitution provide everything they want without the need for winning elections have tried to say that the Constitution can be anything they want it to be, claiming the Constitution is a "living document" amenable to many interpretations. That viewpoint turned the Supreme Court, an institution meant originally to settle disagreements among states and between states and the federal or foreign governments, into an institution that at any time could decide not only that some laws were unconstitutional but could also decide *what it wanted the laws to be*, a viewpoint far removed from the idea that people select their representatives, and the representatives pass the laws that govern all of them.

You've seen how the issue works. Once or twice a year, the national media tell us how the Supreme Court has ruled that some law is or is not constitutional, and then go on to explain how things will be from now on. In the past, police arrest procedure, abortion laws, and gay sex have been just a few of the issues turned completely around by the court. Once the decision is announced, few people are aware that Congress has not done a thing, the president has signed no bill into law, but suddenly our lives are changed by the votes of no more than nine justices—and usually just five. Like most Americans, you probably accept this as the proper functioning of a major part of our national government as laid out in the United States Constitution. But the facts are quite different. There's an excellent argument that the Supreme Court was never meant to overturn the laws of Congress, and certainly never meant to arrogate to itself the power of simply declaring what the law would henceforth be in every state in the union.

And there's that tough question about conservatives and their "cult" of the constitution: are the people who've served on the Supreme Court since 1940 *really* smarter than Thomas Jefferson, James Madison, and everybody between them and Oliver Wendell Holmes? It's one thing to say the liberals from 1940 to 1990 were right and found a lot of rights that had been hidden in the Constitution like so many Easter eggs, but it's another thing to say that everyone who read the Constitution for 170 years had his head up his butt, and *only* these guys were smart enough to figure it all out. In fact, it's pretty much impossible that only justices serving from 1940–90 knew what was really in the Constitution; the odds are much greater that those decisions were anomalous and the earlier decisions were on the right track.

"Interpreting" the Constitution assumes that there are great difficulties in understanding what the framers wanted, as if they wrote in some language from another solar system; but that's not the problem. The problem has been finding ways to justify liberal ideas *despite* the clear meaning of the Constitution.

If you go through Supreme Court decisions from the period around the Warren court (1953–69), you'll be surprised at how many had to be "based" on the Constitution's Commerce Clause or the Bill of Rights "as adopted" through the Fourteenth Amendment to apply to the states. But if the Constitution really needed "interpreting," then huge swaths of it would have to be reworked because of the "problem" of understanding what the framers meant. But the framers were extremely clear in setting out our Constitution—which is why it's actually so difficult for activists to find cover for their interpretations in it. So much of the Constitution is so clear, even to a layperson, that the finagling has to be forced not through a couple of articles, amendments, or paragraphs, but through a few *phrases* that can be taken out of context and twisted to fit the liberal agenda.

Now do me this favor—*look* at the Constitution. You don't even have to read the whole thing, short as it is. What's the first thing it talks about? Certainly not the Supreme Court. After its short preamble,[2] it goes right into the structure of the Congress and what it is expected to do. Why? Because the legislative branch is the closest (through elections and communication) to the *real* sovereign, the people of the United States. Then in Article II, the Constitution deals with the executive branch and what the president is expected to do. After all that, Article III deals with the Supreme Court. Now, still without reading them, just look at the first three sections. Article I, setting up Congress, is about twice as long as Article II, which deals with the presidency. Article II is about twice as long as Article III, which sets up the Supreme Court. Why, if the founders wanted the Supreme Court to be able to override the will of the people anytime it wanted, would its formation be located beneath the Congress and presidency in the Constitution? If that were what they wanted, wouldn't it have been easier to have avoided all those difficult decisions about democracy and the mechanics of a republic and simply have nominated a bunch of old lawyers, given them all the power, and gone home?

Even better, if the founders wanted the Supreme Court to be able to override the other two branches, wouldn't they have *mentioned* it in the Constitution? At no place in the Constitution does it outline the court's power to nullify what the other two branches have done. Article III sets up the Supreme Court, and backers of the liberal justices point to a couple of phrases such as "all Cases, in Law and Equity, arising under this Constitution," but that refers to deciding cases *according* to the Constitution, not using cases to decide *what the Constitution means*. Even a superficial look at the document shows how much time and effort the framers spent considering how Congress and the president would be chosen and exactly what their powers are; why would they put the power to override all that in a few words that are simply a description of the Supreme Court's purpose, which is to untangle disagreements between the federal government and the states and other nations, and between states themselves?

Consider how the framers must have felt. Here they were, just a few years away from being under the crushing power of the British Empire with its arbitrary rulings by a distant power. Why would they set up the

---

[2] When I was a child, students were required to memorize the preamble while in middle school. Thanks to the Supreme Court's takeover of education, students aren't even expected to learn how to *spell* "constitution."

same arbitrary power over themselves to be wielded by nine men[3] who can't be thrown out of office?

The point of this book is to show you how the court "interpreted" the Constitution into a tool for overwhelming the sovereignty of the people. I'm going to go through what these justices actually said and wrote and show you where they made their decisions against the framers, and why the results have often been the opposite of what the writers of these majority opinions claimed they would be.

These actions cannot be defended by a rational argument—why go to the trouble of electing legislatures and have them pass laws if judges are just going to do whatever the hell they want? The idea is that Congress passes laws with the input of voters, then hands things over to an executive branch (with only one elected official—the president) to enforce the laws. Finally comes the judicial branch, which, under the original Constitution, didn't even have the ability to rule on the constitutionality of a law. That was changed in the famous *Marbury v. Madison,* a case well-known to every schoolchild back when schoolchildren actually studied history. In the case, which dealt with the appointment of low-level judges in the District of Columbia in 1803, Chief Justice John Marshall established the concept of constitutional review of the other branches by the Supreme Court. I want to show how the entire concept was based on a fallacy. See if you can spot the disconnect in a key sentence from the case:

> Between these alternatives there is no middle ground. The Constitution is either a superior, paramount law, unchangeable by ordinary means, or it is on a level with ordinary legislative acts, and like other acts, is alterable when the legislature shall please to alter it.[4]

Well, gosh, a citizen might say after reading that, "We sure don't want the legislature to be able to pass laws that it knows are unconstitutional and then have no way to stop it, so it sure is good that the Supreme Court is there to help out." But on further reflection, that citizen should think, "Wait a minute—maybe Congress shouldn't have the power to change the Constitution whenever it wants to, but why should the Supreme Court,

---

[3] Although the court now has nine justices, *that* is not mentioned in the Constitution, either.

[4] Marbury v. Madison, 5 U.S. 137 (1803).

without even the defense of being chosen by the people, have the right to change the Constitution whenever *it* wants to?" The big difference is that even if Congress could pass laws that breach the Constitution, the people still have the power to vote them out of office—something not allowed with the Supreme Court.

Let's say we admit the Supreme Court has the power to decide what is constitutional and what isn't. At least we should be reassured that the court must follow the reasoning and letter of the law in making its decisions. If nothing else, the citizens can be protected by the laws Congress passes—if the Supreme Court rules them constitutional. And that seemed to work for a while, until the jurists figured a way around that: legal pragmatism. The idea of legal pragmatism is that while the courts may not always follow the *letter* of the law, they would be guided by the *spirit* of the law and rule in a way that would be "fair" even if it technically was not "legal."

You've probably heard that argument so many times in modern America that you don't even know there's another side to the story, so let me phrase it another way: what if the Supreme Court said it would not pay attention to the Constitution, the laws Congress passed, or what the voters of America desired, but rather would base its decisions on what the Spirit of the Sacred White Buffalo told them as the judges sat around a campfire and chewed magic mushrooms? Would *that* seem rational to you?

This I-want-it-so-I'm-calling-it-constitutional attitude was first labeled "judicial activism" in 1947.[5] Like other terms that show liberalism for what it is, liberals first tried to deny it and then tried to flip the meaning of the term to apply it to conservatives who believe the Constitution means what it says. A recent law journal article tried to place the description of judicial activism on Supreme Court decisions made *before* justices started making up stuff and proclaiming it constitutional.

> During this period [before the abrupt 1937 change in the court's actions], the Court's alleged "activism" (had the phrase been known) took several forms. The Court invented a constitutional right to contract and granted full-faith-and-credit protection to interstate corporations...the Court restricted labor interests and promoted industrial development.[6]

---

[5] Arthur Schlesinger Jr., "The Supreme Court: 1947," *Fortune*, January 1947.

[6] Craig Green, "An Intellectual History of Judicial Activism," *Emory Law Journal* 58, no. 5 (2009): 1209–10.

Yeah, that was some nasty judicial activism—except that Article I, Section 10, of the Constitution says states may not pass any "Law impairing the Obligation of Contracts," which pretty much puts the right to contract in the Constitution. Then Article IV, Section 1, says, "Full faith and Credit shall be given in each state to the public Acts, Records, and Judicial Proceedings of every other State," which means that state laws regarding corporations[7] should be honored by other states. The complaint about restricting labor interests likely refers to the court's rulings that federal laws could not simply set hours worked in all states, nor could they allow labor unions monopoly power to speak for all employees of a certain craft, such as one labor union given power by the government to deal with carmakers to set wages, while the carmakers had no choice of being nonunion or dealing with another union. Here, the court looked at the Constitution's strict list of what Congress can do (Article I, Section 8), found nothing in it about labor laws, and then looked at the Tenth Amendment, which reserves all "powers not delegated to the United States by the Constitution" to the states and people. Easy call—except that didn't suit the way liberals wanted the country run, so they decided to agree on what seemed like a nice thing to do and then claim it was in the Constitution, and if wasn't there, they decided at least there are "penumbras formed by emanations" of rights in the Constitution that make their decision legal (as we'll see in *Griswold v. Connecticut* and *Roe v. Wade*).

Much of the change in what the Constitution is supposed to say is due to decisions made by the US Supreme Court from 1937 to 1995, especially the court headed by Chief Justice Earl Warren from 1953 to 1969. The man who brought the court to the depths we knew in the middle of the twentieth century was a politician, not a judge. In fact, he had *never* been a judge before being stuck on the high court as its leader in 1953.[8] Choosing a man who'd never been a judge at any level of government—from justice of the peace to appeals judge—to be chief justice of the United States might seem like a strange thing to do, and it was, as odd as making a Little League pitcher a starter for the New York Yankees. But the reason for doing

---

[7] The term "incorporation" comes from the Latin *in corpore*, meaning in body or substance. In other words, a corporation is a person under the law, so treating them with the same laws as humans is realistic.

[8] "Here was Warren, assuming the role of the nation's top judge, with no previous experience as a bench officer, at either the state or federal level." Roger M. Grace, "Earl Warren, Norwegian American," Great Norwegians, http://www.mnc.net/norway/warren.htm.

so was as old as the United States: pure politics. In fact, the man who made this appointment was one of the few presidents to be elected without having ever run for any other office: Dwight Eisenhower.

What you may not have learned in school is that Earl Warren was on the national political stage four years before Eisenhower; in 1948, when he was governor of California, he was the Republican nominee for vice president. He planned to run for president in 1952, since his former running mate, Thomas Dewey, had lost both in 1944 and 1948. But along came Dwight Eisenhower, who was a national hero because of his position as allied commander in Europe during World War II. He took the nomination, and in order to get the support of the California delegation and to keep the three-term California governor out of the game, Ike promised Warren the first available opening on the US Supreme Court. Unfortunately for Eisenhower, that opening came early in his administration, and it was the position of chief justice.

One major problem with Earl Warren as a jurist was his background as a politician. While a judge may feel a need to weigh the legality or rationality of opposing arguments in a case and choose the one that best matches the stated law, a politician put in the highest judicial position in America will instead think like a politician: *I've got a lot of power here, so how am I going to use it to reward my friends and hurt my enemies?* The way to do that is to use the law as one wishes rather than thinking or acting in an objective way about the law.

The Warren court decided that dozens of rights existed under the Constitution that hadn't been recognized before, and it got rid of more than a few that *were* in the Constitution. As the liberal flagship *The New York Times* noted in 2007, liberals think the Supreme Court must "protect ideals of equality and liberty in light of the nation's entire history, rather than legalistically parsing the original understanding of the Constitution."[9] But an intelligent observer might wonder, *How can this be?* The parts of the Constitution these changes came from are the same today as they were in 1787. Were they wrong before, and only the Warren court was smart enough to see that? Were the members of that court truly more intelligent than the framers of the Constitution *and* everyone who served on the Supreme Court and in Congress for the next 160 years? And if they were

---

[9] Jeffrey Rosen, "The Dissenter," *New York Times Magazine*, September 23, 2007.

more intelligent, why didn't their decisions result in a better America than existed before?

To give you an idea of how liberals think, a recent book on the court was titled *Justice for All: Earl Warren and the Nation He Made*. Made? Supreme Court justices were never meant to go around remaking this nation—that's the job of the people, *then* the Congress. Even the president is out of that loop. Where did liberals get the idea that the court is allowed to remake the nation as it wishes on any given day?

The key change in how the court worked was to stop thinking of the Supreme Court as above politics and instead consider it as just another way to achieve liberal political ends. That was made clear in the 1930s when Franklin Roosevelt threatened to "pack" the court when it wouldn't do his political bidding and instead insisted on following the Constitution. With no constitutional limit to the number of Supreme Court Justices, Roosevelt decided to name six new members loyal to him, raising the total to fifteen. Those six would vote with liberal justices already in FDR's pocket and guarantee wins, whatever the Constitution said. The uproar from the public forced even the popular FDR to back down, but the court suddenly decided to start ruling more in Roosevelt's favor.[10]

Liberals have always known the Constitution is opposed to almost all the socialistic claptrap they worship, and that's why they demand that justices "interpret the Constitution in light of the entire history of the nation, and not just in light of the Constitution's drafting history."[11] But if the Constitution is open to interpretation and change, why are all federal officials and members of the armed services still sworn into office promising to "preserve, protect, and defend the Constitution"?[12] Are they swearing to protect and defend any changes liberals think of? And doesn't "preserve" mean *not* changing? If the justices can choose anything from the entire history of the nation as an "interpretation" of the Constitution, doesn't that mean they can do anything they want, considering how many different historical occurrences they can choose to "interpret"? Such silliness leads to quotes such as the one from Justice John Paul Stevens that "the notion that

---

[10] This abrupt change was known afterward as the "switch in time saves nine," that is, nine justices. Why enough judges started voting differently to make FDR happy is something of a mystery. I've always figured the administration had some justice's daughter in the trunk of a Packard or something.

[11] Rosen, "The Dissenter."

[12] U.S. Const. art. II, § 1. This oath was required for any president but has spread to the military and the rest of the federal government.

judges should treat all racial classifications alike...'doesn't make *sense*.'"[13] But if all racial classifications *aren't* to be treated alike, who decides *how* they should be treated? How does one load the dice to get the "proper" treatment for various groups? Rather than simply treat the matter as a democracy would, by not giving any ethnic group extra consideration under the law, liberals want to decide *who* gets extra help and *how much* extra help they receive, all without ever referring to the Constitution. Somehow this makes sense to them: that equality can only result from carefully chosen *in*equality, and that somehow they are the only persons who know how this inequality should be handed out.

If my critique seems overwrought—and I admit I do get worked up about this—think of how things would be if a physicist decided that rather than going along with natural laws, he would simply make up his own. After all, how much easier the world and geometry class would be if ϖ were equal to exactly 3.000 instead of the much clumsier 3.1415926535...! Likewise, Supreme Court justices can't simply decide what they *want* the Constitution to read; they must actually read it and decide based on the words and meaning therein; otherwise there is *no way* to know how this country is supposed to work. *Apres le loi, le deluge.* Once the court decides to "interpret" the Constitution, it can pretty much do anything it wants. And the next court can do what *it* wants, *ad infinitum.* Before long, the Constitution is twisted completely out of shape, and you're stuck with the impossible situation we're in today.

That interpretive viewpoint had taken over the national media by the time Earl Warren died in 1974, so much so that the obituary written in *Time* magazine was headlined "Earl Warren's Way: 'Is It Fair?'" After mentioning the one-man one-vote decision on legislative districting, school desegregation, and "the broadening of criminal suspects' rights," the story notes:

> Yet Warren was not an ideologue or radical. Rather he was a pragmatist who came to the bench with no preconceived notion or grand design, no strongly held or elaborately developed theory of the society or even the law itself. He did right as he learned to see the right; the key word was learned.[14]

---

[13] Rosen, "The Dissenter."

[14] "The Law: Earl Warren's Way: Is It Fair?," *Time*, July 22, 1974, http://www.time.com/time/magazine/article/0,9171,942946,00.html.

11

Well, what's wrong with that? I mean, don't we all try to be fair, and isn't it better that we have no "preconceived notion or grand design"? In answer, let's say you hire a highly respected architect to build a skyscraper. He comes to the first meeting and you ask him what he has in mind for the building and he answers, "Well, I have no preconceived notion or grand design. I plan to learn as I go along." After overcoming your shock, you may say, "Well, at least you'll observe the laws of physics and not build anything that might collapse and kill hundreds of people, right?" To which the highly respected architect replies, "I may or may not observe the laws of physics. Instead, I plan to do what I think is fair. Some people may die, and you may not receive what you thought you wanted, but I plan to be pragmatic and progressive, and that's even better than following all those little details."

This is about the point where you would chase the highly respected architect out of your office with a baseball bat, but we weren't as lucky with Earl Warren and his minions. Seventeen years before that glowing report on progressive pragmatism, *Time*'s editors had more sense in reviewing the first four years of the Warren court's decisions: *"Potential damage to the continuity and structure of the law* sobered many observers who felt the instinct to cheer the net effect of the [Warren court] decisions"[15] (italics added). Later in that paragraph the writer mentions that a key decision of the court rested "on only the barest recognizable relationship between the law and the findings." The article continues: "Confusing practice, no matter in what cause, can only damage the shape of a legal system painstakingly built, block by block, with the accumulated wisdom of the ages." I've been telling you the Supreme Court clearly acted out of bounds for half a century; here's a top reporter on the subject, working for a highly respected news organization, saying the same thing. And he was right, but the damage had been done. While Americans were rebuilding their lives and the economy after the war, the Warren court was already making the decisions that would have us looking back to a time when things were so nice—the time *before* those decisions took effect. The Warren court had decided that when the Constitution and Congress opposed whatever the hell the justices wanted, whatever the hell the justices wanted would win. By 1975, the court would be so openly dismissive of the law and public opinion that longtime Justice William O. Douglas would be quoted as saying, "I won't resign while

---

[15] "The Temple Builder," *Time*, July 1, 1957.

12

there's a breath in my body—until we get a Democratic president."[16] So much for being disinterested, fair, and above the pull of partisan politics.

With that said, let's take a look at how fewer than a dozen men did more damage to our country than Nazi Germany, Imperial Japan, and the USSR combined could do in almost a century of effort.

---

[16] "Douglas Finally Leaves the Bench," *Time*, November 24, 1975.

IT'S A FREE COUNTRY, AIN'T IT? WICKARD V. FILBURN (1942)

It's not hard to decide where to start in looking at the perversion of freedom the Supreme Court has committed, if you do it on a wholesale basis. In the retail trade of selling out America, there were a few decisions earlier, but the big fire sale on freedom begins with Franklin D. Roosevelt's New Deal in the 1930s.

While the Supreme Court had made foolish or incorrect decisions before, an actual conspiracy to subvert the Constitution itself didn't really get underway until Roosevelt's legislative programs kept being sunk by the Supreme Court, which declared that they were intrusive, ignored people's and states' rights, and took over large sections of the economy in totalitarian ways—which they did. Neither FDR nor his fellow Democrats in Congress gave a hoot about this—they had decided socialism was the wave of the future and it was time to start swimming in it before the Soviet Union, Nazi Germany, or Sweden beat us to it. So, like most bullies, FDR started threatening the court itself. As mentioned earlier, Roosevelt simply threatened to get Congress to seat another six more malleable justices on the court so he would have a solid majority willing to rubber-stamp everything he wanted. That failed, but for some reason, the court decided in 1937 to start approving what Roosevelt wanted, and Chief Justice Owen Roberts started allowing FDR full rein.

Within five years, the country almost wiped out property rights with *Wickard v. Filburn*.[17] *Wickard* dealt with something that doesn't interest liberals much: the right to do what you wish with what you own, something that would seem to be a crucial right in a capitalistic society.

Filburn was a poor farmer in Ohio who stepped into the buzz saw of Roosevelt's Agricultural Adjustment Act of 1938. Like other socialistic claptrap, it promised much and delivered nothing at huge cost to the people it claimed to be helping. The idea was that some genius in a government office in Washington could figure out *just how much* of each product should be raised by each farmer and rancher to help raise prices. That's right—they simply decided that free enterprise and open markets couldn't work as well as socialist bureaucrats scratching their ears with well-chewed pencils. Of course, many people in the 1930s felt that way, but every one of them had to do so by ignoring the fact that the government's own mismanagement of the money supply had made the Depression so vicious.[18]

Mr. Filburn was awarded an "allotment" of 11.1 acres for his wheat crop, as long as he didn't bring in more than 20.1 bushels of wheat per acre. Filburn went along with this. Let me repeat—*Filburn went along with the federal law.* His mistake was in figuring that, hey, I understand that the federal law controls anything I might want to sell as a farmer, but certainly what I raise for my own use doesn't affect the national economy. So he planted another 11.9 acres with wheat to feed his chickens and cattle and produce flour for his own family. That's it. Believe it or not, this became a Supreme Court case.

Before I get into details, take time to note the bureaucrat-technocrat viewpoint, believing that sure enough, the Brain Trust in Washington could figure out exactly what each farmer in America should raise, down to the tenth of an acre and tenth of a bushel. To give you some idea of the idiocy of this concept, let's look at an article in *The New York Times* from the week the decision in Filburn's case was handed down, several years after he was first charged by the government. Now remember, Filburn was sued up to the Supreme Court level because he planted 11.9 more acres of wheat than

---

[17] 317 U.S. 111 (1942).

[18] The federal government, which took over the money supply in 1913, kept expanding it through the 1920s until it found that if it printed money faster than the production of goods and services increased, it caused inflation, which in this case showed up as a booming stock market as well as higher prices elsewhere. When it decided to cut back in the summer of 1929, it did so by slashing the money supply by *30 percent* and keeping it there. No wonder prices dropped in the Depression! But of course, the government always finds something other to blame than itself, such as greedy capitalists or bad weather.

the Agriculture Department allowed. The idea was that, gee, if we let just anyone plant as much of a crop as they want, production will go crazy, and prices will plunge. Now check out this front-page headline from the *Times* on November 19, 1942: "DAIRY PRODUCTS RATIONING IS ASKED BY WICKARD TO MEET BIG DEMAND."[19] Note that Wickard, the guy involved in Filburn's lawsuit, is the secretary of agriculture. And also notice that after five years of monkey business of "scientifically" controlling supply and demand, so many farmers have been beaten down to nothing that now there aren't *enough* farm products to go around. The Associated Press, which reported the story, misses the irony. "Faced with war demands beyond the apparent ability of farmers to supply," it begins, the government "is expected soon to recommend civilian rationing of cheese and butter, fluid milk in larger cities, and a curtailment of manufacture of ice cream." Not only did the armed forces need more, but Allied nations were on the handout line, and besides, "civilian demands were reported increasing also, owing to shortages of meat and rising incomes."[20] The rising incomes, of course, resulted from continued government-caused inflation as the government printed more money to buy war machinery. Besides, "dairymen face[d] a growing shortage of labor, equipment, and transportation facilities..."[21] Like, duh, dude; I mean, you beat every farmer who dares to raise a bit more of anything than you allow them—don't you think they'll be cutting back on production, labor, and equipment? Even better is the headline, so typical of government action: "Rationing Is Asked...to Meet Big Demand." Yeah, rather than allow the price to increase to cool demand a bit, you want to ration the results of your own idiocy, leading to the inevitable black marketing and diversion from supplies. But of course, the advantage to all this is that government stooges can claim none of this was their fault—it's all those lazy farmers and black marketers who are to blame!

But back to the results of the government's stupidity the *first* time around. The Supreme Court, through Justice Jackson, tried to explain what was going on, by saying, "to avoid surpluses and shortages...":

Within prescribed limits and by prescribed standards the Secretary of Agriculture is directed to ascertain and proclaim

---

[19] *New York Times*, November 19, 1942.

[20] *Id.*

[21] "Dairy Product Rationing Is Asked by Wickard to Meet Big Demand," *New York Times*, November 19, 1942.

each year a national acreage allotment for the next crop of wheat, which is then apportioned to the states and their counties, and is eventually broken up into allotments for individual farms.[22]

Justice Jackson's opinion states that this would be a slam-dunk if Filburn had sold the wheat, but consuming it on his own farm—was that really under government control? As is typical, Jackson admits that under current law, it *isn't*: "Even today, when this power has been held to have great latitude, there is no decision of this Court that such activities may be regulated where *no part of the product is intended for interstate commerce* or intermingled with the subjects thereof"[23] (italics added). But, as you will see in later cases, that is merely the slightest nod to reality before the court goes ahead and rips up the Constitution. Jackson then spends the next five pages explaining that the court has never before decided to exert such power and then spends a few pages explaining the mechanics of the world wheat market.

But remember, Filburn *never put his wheat on any market.* He raised it for personal consumption by his family and his livestock. That did not make any difference to the court. "But if we assume that it is never marketed," Jackson states, the wheat "supplies a need of the man who grew it which would otherwise be reflected by purchases in the open market. Home-grown wheat in this sense competes with wheat in commerce. The stimulation of commerce is a use of the regulatory function quite as definitely as prohibitions or restrictions thereon." So the high-water mark was met—even something you produced for your own use was under government control. The Soviet Union's only addition to this was that they removed the fig leaf of private ownership of land. Otherwise, it was the same—we plan what you will plant and reap, and you'd better do it, pal. We should thank the Lord that the federal government didn't make it illegal to *think* about planting extra wheat.

Filburn's fine for raising too much wheat was $111, but the aftereffects continued for decades. The court's decision that government had this power was based on the Commerce Clause in the Constitution, Article I, Section 8, paragraph 3: "To regulate Commerce with foreign nations, among the several States, and with the Indian Tribes." The court had no

---

[22] Wickard v. Filburn, 317 U.S. 111, 114 (1942).

[23] *Id.* at 120.

problem deciding it could stretch "among"[24] to mean "inside just one" simply because it wanted to. As I've noted before, the Constitution was well written and didn't leave much room for liberals to wiggle out of it. Like a well-built safe cracked by burglars, it's clear where the pressure was applied—in the Commerce Clause, the "Necessary and Proper" Clause of Article I, and the Due Process Clause of the Fourteenth Amendment.[25] The Commerce Clause was so stretched that when the court finally pulled back on it in 1995, liberals were "shocked" that it wouldn't allow the Commerce Clause to cover carrying a gun in a city's school zone. Not the sale of a gun, or carrying a gun to protect illegal drug sales, but just having one, as if carrying a pistol in Texas would magically affect business activities in New Hampshire.[26]

I've spent many years wondering why liberals think as they do in economic matters, and my current theory is that liberals are indeed smarter than *most* people, but not as smart as *some* people. They are just smart enough to think that, hey, I need to step in and take over before this chump screws up his life, so I'll get a law passed that tells him what he can and can't do. The problem with this is that liberals never seem to make that next jump and realize that, in the scheme of things, *they* aren't smart enough to figure it out either. That's because the market, the "invisible hand," as Adam Smith[27] called it, is smarter than *all* of us.

There's another reason the market works so well. It's said that 90 percent of all new businesses fail; certainly most movies lose money, and most wildcat oil wells are dusters. So how do industries survive? Because someone is occasionally right, and that particular venture makes tons of money. Plus, if there is a technical or economic advancement involved, most of the rest of us learn to change to take advantage of it. Out of the thousands of inventions, new businesses, new locations, new techniques, new movies and

---

[24] If you think "among" can mean "inside," note this from the *Associated Press Stylebook* (1984): "The maxim that *between* introduces two items and *among* introduces more than two covers most questions about how to use these words..." That is, among refers to commerce *between* one state and more than one other, not what goes on *inside* a single state.

[25] For most "big government" issues. In criminal law, the court's fingerprints are generally found in the Fourth, Fifth, and Sixth Amendments, but remember that those were written to apply only to the federal government; the Fourteenth Amendment is used as a way to apply them to the states.

[26] United States v. Lopez, 514 U.S. 549 (1995). This occurred in San Antonio, Texas. The idiocy of this case is that Texas had a proper law against such an offense, but of course the Congress had to show how proschool and antigun it was by passing the Gun-Free School Zones Act of 1990, which it claimed was justified by the Commerce Clause.

[27] Scottish proto-economist who wrote *The Wealth of Nations* in 1776.

songs developed every day in this country, only a few are successful, and fewer than that are wildly successful. But those are enough to keep things going in style.

Where liberals go wrong is that *nobody knows which ones will be successful ahead of time.* That means no one can sit in a government office and decide what ideas to fund, markets to expand or contract, businesses to open or close. Until some super-quantum computer comes along, the market is all we have to apportion the resources of society efficiently. The problem is that people look at success with hindsight and think they could have predicted it. Bill Gates? Why sure, just give someone the operating system for 90 percent of the home computers on earth, and he'll get rich—*but which operating system was it going to be?* How did we know Bill Gates would be able to take the idea and develop it properly? Yeah, he's a real smart guy, but there are thousands of guys just as smart—maybe hundreds of thousands—and most of them are just moderately successful. How could we have known, in 1929, that fungus would lead to antibiotics? Alexander Bell beat Elisha Gray to the Patent Office with the concept for the telephone by five hours—how could you have handicapped that? Quick, what kind of car will dominate in fifty years? Hybrid? Diesel? Solar? None at all?

So Mr. Filburn lost his case, but his loss was minimal compared to the huge loss suffered by our economy over the next six decades. After *Wickard v. Filburn,* there was nothing either Congress or the court didn't think they could control.

"EXCLUDING" THE CONSTITUTION
MAPP V. OHIO (1961)

Today the case of *Mapp v. Ohio* is known as the one that brought us the exclusionary rule. That rule, as most television watchers know, is one that excludes from a criminal case any evidence found while a law was being violated. Most people think this rule has been around almost forever, but in fact it all sprang from the fevered brows of the nine Warren court justices.

Until 1961, police officers could face punishment or even criminal charges for gathering evidence in an illegal way, but almost no one was crazy enough to think that the evidence thus gathered should be barred from the courtroom. After all, it was evidence. For instance, it's illegal to steal a car, but there's no rule that requires a stolen car be mashed into a cube simply because a person acted illegally in obtaining it; instead, the person who stole it is punished, and the car is returned to the owner or sold at auction.

Mapp v. Ohio is probably the one Supreme Court ruling on criminal law that angers the most people. If you hear that someone avoided conviction on a "legal technicality," it's probably *Mapp* that's to blame. After all, look at what we're talking about—the exclusionary rule is only brought into play *if the suspect is clearly guilty.* There's never a time when a person as innocent as last night's snowfall is facing wrongful prosecution and the rule is used; it is used for people whose guilt was proved by evidence police collected, and *then the lawyers get the guilty party off.* No wonder it makes people so mad. And you're going to be even angrier when you see how *Mapp v.*

Ohio led to the exclusionary rule. It's as if the Supreme Court knew what it wanted to do and just waited for the right case to ram it through. Which, of course, it did.

For attorneys and others interested in the law, it is highly instructive to read both the famous case of *Mapp v. Ohio*[28] and the less well-known *Mapp v. State*[29] that preceded it. *Mapp v. State* was decided by the Supreme Court of Ohio in early 1960, and it clearly raised constitutional issues. However, those issues dealt with the obscenity laws of the day, not search and seizure. Let me repeat that—this was an *obscenity* case, not a search-and-seizure test of the Fourth Amendment. Looking at the state of Ohio's version, *Mapp v. State* reads as an obscenity case from the first paragraph of its opinion ("defendant knew at the time she is charged with having possessed them that they represented lewd and lascivious books and pictures"[30]) to the final substantive paragraph ("If anyone looks at a book and finds it lewd, he is forthwith, under this legislation, guilty of a serious crime"[31]).

Now let's look at the US Supreme Court's case. All that obscenity law is dispensed with in a two-sentence first paragraph, and then the opinion of Justice Tom Clark starts presenting a very different story. Three Cleveland police officers show up at Dollree Mapp's home looking for a bombing suspect and gambling paraphernalia; she refuses them entry for lack of search warrant; another four officers arrive three hours later, and the police force their way in.[32] "Having secured their own entry…the officers, in this highhanded manner, broke into the hall."[33] When Miss Mapp took what one officer claimed was a warrant (never confirmed) and stuffed it into her dress, "they handcuffed appellant because she had been 'belligerent' in resisting their official rescue of the 'warrant' from her person."[34] This emotional narrative was nowhere to be found in *Mapp v. State*; Justice Clark's law clerks had been working overtime finding background material while he "was attempting to mold a relatively routine obscenity case into a search and seizure landmark."[35]

---

[28] Mapp v. Ohio, 367 U.S. 643 (1961).

[29] Mapp v. State, 166 N.E. 2d 387 (1960).

[30] *Id.*, at 388.

[31] *Id.* at 391.

[32] Mapp v. Ohio, 367 U.S. 643, 644 (1961).

[33] *Id.*.

[34] *Id.* at 644-45.

[35] Dennis Dorin, "Marshaling Mapp: Justice Tom Clark's Role in Mapp v. Ohio's Extension of the Exclusionary Rule to State Searches and Seizures," 52 (2001) *Case W. Res. L. Rev.*, 401, 423.

The Ohio Supreme Court had indeed wanted a law held unconstitutional, but it was the state's obscenity law, which seemed to require only that obscene materials be in one's possession, without making it clear that the person even knew what they contain.[36] However, the Ohio Constitution said no law could be held unconstitutional if more than one judge voted *not* to find it so,[37] and in this case, three voted against it.[38] Interestingly, had they reversed the obscenity law, the exclusionary rule as we know it today might not have been—or it certainly would not have been *Mapp v. Ohio* that made it so.

In the dissent to *Mapp v. State*, Ohio Supreme Court Judge Herbert does touch on the Fourth Amendment issues (technically, the parallel issues in Article I, Section 14, of the Ohio Constitution[39]), but quickly points out that even he would not have voted in favor of an exclusionary rule in all instances. He does say that in the case before him, the law that allows evidence obtained by unlawful search "seems to me to be far too comprehensive and susceptible to abuse by police and prosecution authorities."[40] But after that paragraph, Judge Herbert moves on to discuss the obscenity laws of the day, and only in the final paragraph does he say "the Lindway rule...should be modified and clarified so that there will no longer be a judicial stamp of approval on the use of unlawful means to justify and [sic] end result."[41]

After reading that state case, the federal case, *Mapp v. Ohio,* is almost a non sequitur, as if two women named Mapp had been accused of different crimes in different locations. In his opinion, Justice Clark begins by stating that "appellant stands convicted of knowingly having had in her possession and under her control certain lewd and lascivious books, pictures, and photographs in violation of Section 2905.4 of Ohio's Revised Code."[42] But Justice Clark then quotes the Ohio Supreme Court's opinion that the conviction was based on evidence seized unlawfully during a search of the

---

[36] Mapp v. State, 166 N.E. 2d 387, 391 (1960).

[37] *Id.* at 391 (quoting Article IV, Section 2 of the Constitution of Ohio).

[38] *Id.* (noting that Justices Taft, Peck, Herbert, and Bell favored finding the law unconstitutional, but Justices Matthias, Zimmerman, and Chief Justice Weygandt did not).

[39] *Id.* at 391-92.

[40] *Id.* at 392 (pointing out that the case on which the court based its opinion, State v. Lindway, 2 N.E. 2d 490, involved manufacturing bombs, and stating that "...neither Constitution nor state law was intended to provide security for such dangerous enemies of our public peace.")

[41] *Id.* at 394.

[42] Mapp v. Ohio, 367 U.S. 643 (1961).

defendant's home.[43] From that point, we are off on a sleigh ride aimed toward the Land of Evidence Exclusion.

Justice Clark spends the next *seventeen pages* justifying his decision to turn an obscenity case into the epitome of exclusionary-rule cases. His only sop to the real case is a quick footnote early on that says, "Other issues have been raised on this appeal but, in the view we have taken of the case, they need not be decided. Although appellant…did not insist that Wolf [the 1949 federal case allowing admission of illegally seized evidence] be over-ruled, the amicus curiae…did urge the Court to overrule Wolf."[44] What this meant was that Miss Mapp's own attorneys hadn't asked for the exclu-sionary rule, but Clark was going to provide it anyway![45]

The belief that Tom Clark twisted the case to suit his desires to change the Constitution might be nothing but surmise except for a couple of sources. One is an excellent law review article by University of North Carolina Law Professor Emeritus Dennis Dorin, "Marshaling Mapp: Justice Tom Clark's Role in Mapp v. Ohio's Extension of the Exclusionary Rule to State Searches and Seizures."[46] Another is an article based on a 1983 speech by Supreme Court Justice Potter Stewart, who was present when it all hap-pened.[47] Both contain evidence that Tom Clark had an agenda far beyond the fate of defendant Dollree Mapp. That *amicus curiae* brief by the ACLU, for instance, is twenty pages long. Only in the final three paragraphs does it ask that the Wolf ruling be overturned, *and Wolf* is the one that allowed courts to hold on to evidence even if it was illegally discovered.[48]

---

[43] *Id.*

[44] *Id.*at 646, FN3. If ever there was a case with its feet nailed to the floor by the court, it was Wolf v. Colorado, 338 U.S. 25 (1949). Justice Frankfurter's opinion that state officials could not be forced to exclude evidence by federal order was straightforward, clear, and stated in the first two paragraphs of the opinion:

The notion that the "due process of law" guaranteed by the Fourteenth Amendment is shorthand for the first eight amendments of the Constitution and thereby incorporates them has been rejected by this Court again and again, after impressive consideration.

Perhaps one reason Justice Douglas voted to overturn the case in 1949 was the fact that it was the prosecution of a physician for abortion, and legalizing abortion was no doubt already on the court liberals' schedule. Wolf v. People, 187 P.2d 926 (1947).

[45] This sort of thing shows up all the time in Warren court opinions: a quick dismissal of the actual issue in the case, then a settling down to what the court *really* wants to talk about.

[46] Dorin, "Marshaling Mapp," 401.

[47] Potter Stewart, "The Road to Mapp v. Ohio and Beyond: The Origins, Development, and Future of the Exclusionary Rule in Search-and-Seizure Cases," *Colum. L. Rev.* 83 (1983), 1365.

[48] *Id.* at 1367.

That the ACLU's argument was not regarded by the parties as even a remotely important issue in the case was made clear at the oral argument. The appellant's lawyer was asked whether he was requesting the court to overrule the Wolf case, and thus, to exclude the fruits of an illegal search at a state trial. He answered, quite candidly, *that he had never heard of the Wolf case*[49] (italics added).

Because of that, it makes sense that Justice Potter Stewart would say he was shocked when he first saw the proposed opinion. "I immediately wrote [Clark] a note expressing my surprise and questioning the wisdom of overruling an important doctrine in a case in which the issue was not briefed, argued, or discussed by the state courts, by the parties' counsel, or at our conference following the oral argument."[50] Stewart's view, twenty-two years after the decision, was that other justices had held a "rump caucus"[51] to discuss a different basis for the decision. If that doesn't make you believe they had an agenda that preceded the actual case, then you just don't want to believe.

Professor Dorin's view is equally polite and equally disapproving of Justice Tom Clark: "Mapp's search and seizure ruling was a direct product of Clark's extraordinary actions—ones that, in turn, were substantially structured and channeled by a conception of a justice's role to which Clark, perhaps uniquely, adhered."[52] Law professors do not use words such as "extraordinary" and "uniquely" lightly in law review articles. Professor Dorin literally means that Justice Clark's actions in the case were well out of the ordinary and that Clark's view of what a justice should or could do may have never been held by any of his colleagues. Without saying so directly, Dorin implies that Clark is a crooked SOB. He goes on to fit Justice Clark into the school of legal pragmatism by stating that Clark held to three rules as a justice: first was "obedience to the law was the foundation...of the American constitutional system."[53] "Second," Dorin wrote, "this approach did not...require Clark to adhere blindly to past precedents."[54] Clark's third rule was that a "justice should never misconstrue purposely, and thus delib-

---

[49] *Id.* at 1365.

[50] *Id.* at 1368.

[51] *Id.*

[52] Dorin, "Marshaling Mapp," 401, 402.

[53] *Id.* at 403.

[54] *Id.* at 401, 404.

erately water down, precedents."[55] But there are cases in which "intellectual purity might…have to defer to compromise."[56] Let's see—claim you really adhere to the Constitution until you decide you want to change it. Then, if you can't come up with previous court rulings that justify your decision, make the ruling anyway and claim you had precedent even if you didn't. *Mapp* was going to be one of these cases.

Remember, *Mapp* clearly came up to the US Supreme Court as a First Amendment obscenity case. The Ohio Supreme Court had voted four-to-three to strike down the applicable legislation in that state,[57] and the original US Supreme Court conference yielded a unanimous vote on the case, overturning the obscenity law under which Miss Mapp was prosecuted because it "made the mere knowing possession of obscene materials a felony."[58] Having overseen the nine-to-none vote, Chief Justice Earl Warren turns over the writing of the majority opinion to Justice Clark. But keep this in mind: Clark was under orders to write a unanimous decision on an obscenity case, not an evidence case.

Clark actually began to outline an opinion based on the First and Fourteenth Amendments, but "the draft trailed off. It was never developed further."[59] After all, why waste your effort on writing an opinion that simply hewed to the facts of the case when you can make stuff up? Instead Clark "had begun to transform Mapp into a state search and seizure landmark."[60] It was not easy. Clark wanted to develop the exclusionary rule, disallowing any and all evidence police obtained against a defendant in an illegal manner. Clark's law clerks went to work, "but they *could not find a single case* that held, in no uncertain terms, that its exclusionary rule was part of the Fourth Amendment"[61] (italics mine). In other words, it was enough of a stretch that Clark might want to apply the Fourth Amendment to the states, but tying it to an exclusionary rule was just short of preposterous. Yes, the federal government had an exclusionary rule, but it was specifically referred to as derived from the court's supervisory powers over inferior courts,[62] not the Fourth Amendment. That

---

[55] *Id.* at 405.

[56] *Id.*

[57] Mapp v. State, 166 N.E. 2d 387, 391 (1960).

[58] Dorin, "Marshaling Mapp," *401, 413.*

[59] *Id.* at 414.

[60] *Id.*

[61] *Id.* at 415.

[62] But see Amy Coney Barrett, "The Supervisory Power of the Supreme Court," *Colum. L. Rev.* 106 n. 9 (2006) 324, 328, which notes that the Supreme Court did not invoke supervisory power when it decided Weeks v.

meant the Supremes could tell lower federal courts to exclude evidence, but they had absolutely *no authority* to tell states how to do their business.

Of course, almost all that juicy criminal law was in state courts, and the Warren court wanted to control it. Clark's defenders might point to *Weeks v. United States*[63] to defend him. There the court's opinion states: "We therefore reach the conclusion that the letters in question were taken from the house of the accused by an official of the United States...in direct violation of the constitutional rights of the defendant. In holding them and permitting their use upon the trial, we think prejudicial error was committed."[64] But this decision turned on a slim hinge—Weeks's attorney had filed for return of the illegally seized evidence before trial began; because of that, the high court's opinion was that the government had been required to return the papers *before* the trial began and hence could not use the papers as evidence in the trial.[65] A clear exclusionary rule did not exist in 1914, even for the federal government. As for the states, Justice William R. Day's opinion noted, "What remedies the defendant may have against them we need not inquire, as the 4th Amendment is not directed to individual misconduct of [state] officials. Its limitations reach the Federal government and its agencies."[66] Ding! Ding! Ding! Can you hear that, Chief Justice Warren?

Even in 1949, the decision in *Wolf v. Colorado*,[67] while applying the Fourth Amendment to states through the Fourteenth and claiming that security in one's house is "implicit in the concept of ordered liberty,"[68] still shied away from an exclusionary rule for the then obvious reason that it "directly serves only to protect those upon whose person or premises something incriminating has been found."[69] Exactly. *Exactly.* Why have a rule whose sole reason for existence is to let known criminals walk out of court?

Justice Clark's first version of the opinion, in fact, states clearly that the Supreme Court has no right to rule the way he ends up ruling in *Mapp*: "On

United States, 232 U.S. 383 (1914), the first exclusionary rule case. Weeks purported to ground the exclusion of illegally seized evidence in the Fourth Amendment itself. It was not until after McNabb that some justices explained Weeks as an exercise of the court's supervisory power. (Barrett specifically refers to Harlan's dissent in *Mapp* as such an explanation.)

[63] 232 U.S. 383 (1914).

[64] *Id.* at 383, 398.

[65] Stewart, "The Road to Mapp v. Ohio and Beyond," 1365, 1375.

[66] *Weeks*, 232 U.S. at 398.

[67] 338 U.S. 25 (1949).

[68] *Id.* at 27 (quoting Palko v. Connecticut, 302 U.S. 319, 325 [1937]).

[69] *Id.* at 31.

the Fourth Amendment question the Court adheres to the rule announced in *Wolf, supra,* and hence this contention of the applicant is denied."[70] A later opinion decides to overrule *Wolf,* but it is clear that Clark is grabbing at twigs—the draft runs nineteen pages and reads like something written by a first-year law student. A real judge knows that he or she should cite the majority opinion about 95 percent of the time. After all, the majority shows how the case law actually went; quoting from concurrences (judges who agree with the overall ruling but disagree with a part of it) or dissents (what's written by the losing side to explain its vote) doesn't get much accomplished—unless you have a majority on the Supreme Court, and then you can do anything you want. Clark quotes the dissenting opinion in *Harris v. United States*[71] to shore up his belief in a right to privacy, quotes Justice Brandeis's dissent in *Olmstead v. United States,*[72] and is again on the losing side when he quotes the dissent in *Abel v. United States*[73] in a feeble attempt to counter Justice Cardozo's brilliant comment that the bad thing about an exclusionary policy is that "the criminal is to go free because the constable has blundered."[74] Bingo.

Justice Clark's opinion in *Mapp* starts out touching lightly on the precedent of *Boyd v. United States,*[75] but successive drafts bring it to the fore, from page eleven to page three to the first line of his legal interpretation

---

[70] Draft of opinion on Mapp case delivered by Justice Clark (1961), *The Papers of Justice Tom C. Clark,* http://utopia.utexas.edu/explore/clark/view_doc.php?id=a115-01-02&page=2 (site last visited March 26, 2006).

[71] Harris v. United States, 331 U.S. 145 (1960). The right to privacy is "second to none in the Bill of Rights." *Id.* at 157.

[72] Olmstead v. United States, 277 U.S. 438 (1928). "If the government becomes a lawbreaker, it breeds contempt for the law; it invites every man to become a law unto himself; it invites anarchy." *Id.* at 469. At least Justice Holmes in his dissent made clear what Justice Clark could not, thirty-three years later: "There is no body of precedents by which we are bound, and which confines us to logical deduction from established rules. Therefore we must consider the two objects of desire both of which we cannot have and make up our minds which to choose." *Id.* at 470. Holmes saw that there was no way to justify the decision to impose an exclusionary rule; if the court wanted it, it simply had to do it.

[73] Abel v. United States, 362 U.S. 237.

[74] People v. Defore, 150 N.E. 585, 587 (1926). As a comparison, if the IRS figures your taxes incorrectly or issues you a refund check for fifty million bucks, do you get to walk away free? No way, so why have an exclusionary rule that lets criminals walk if the police make a minor error?

[75] 116 U.S. 616 (1886). Interestingly, *Boyd v. United States,* though used as support by Justice Clark, wasn't even a search-and-seizure issue. It was a case, in those pre-income-tax days, involving the nonpayment of import duty on thirty-five cases of plate glass. The federal attorney demanded the defendants turn over an invoice for twenty-nine cases of glass they'd received earlier, then kept the invoice as evidence of the value of the glass in question. Boyd claimed a Fifth Amendment right against use of the invoice as evidence. The court decided that since testimony was not involved, it would put it under the Fourth:
It is our opinion, therefore, that a compulsory production of a man's private papers to establish a criminal charge against him…is within the scope of the fourth amendment to the constitution, in all cases in which a search

of *Mapp*.[76] The fact that *Boyd* fuses the Fourth and Fifth Amendments to get exclusion of evidence by saying it would amount to compelled testimony against oneself, and that the seizure of evidence in the *Mapp* case was not in violation of the Fifth Amendment, is ignored.[77] In fact, Clark concedes *Boyd*'s point, footnotes the Fourth Amendment without the Fifth, quotes Lord Camden's 1765 view against self-accusation that *predated* our Constitution, and having totally run the two amendments together, using what he wished, goes on his way.[78]

The final opinion also made much of the fact that in 1949, the year of *Wolf*, almost two-thirds of the states opposed the exclusionary rule, while when *Mapp* appeared in 1961, more than half endorsed it.[79] This is ruling by baseball score, as if the fact that only Nevada has legalized gambling and prostitution means that the Supreme Court should rule it unconstitutional because of the forty-nine-to-one view of the issue. Besides, those numbers should actually be evidence in favor of *not* forcing the exclusionary rule on the states—if the states are coming around to the exclusionary rule on their own, why require a massive overruling of a much-used case (*Wolf*) and shove exclusion down the throats of a minority of states? If the federal government truly respected the states, as it promises to in the Ninth and Tenth Amendments to the Constitution, it could expect them to see the light eventually, and certainly *Mapp* is no crucial case requiring an instant finding of unconstitutionality (at least regarding the Fourth Amendment), since it could have easily been decided on obscenity grounds.

But Justice Clark got his opinion and a handy six-to-three vote—not the unanimity he could have gotten had he left the case in the First Amendment

---

and seizure would be, because it is a material ingredient, and effects the sole object and purpose of search and seizure. (*Id.* at 622),

[76] See Dorin, "Marshaling Mapp," 418–23 (noting Clark's upgrading of *Boyd* as he gained more confidence in his opinion).

[77] *Id.* at 418. *Boyd v. U.S.* made all this quite clear, had anyone wanted to look:

We have already noticed the intimate relation between the two amendments. They throw great light on each other. For the "unreasonable searches and seizures" condemned in the fourth amendment are almost always made for the purpose of compelling a man to give evidence against himself, which in criminal cases is condemned in the fifth amendment; and compelling a man "in a criminal case to be a witness against himself," which is condemned in the fifth amendment, throws light on the question as to what is an "unreasonable search and seizure" within the meaning of the fourth amendment. And we have been unable to perceive that the seizure of a man's private books and papers to be used in evidence against him is substantially different from compelling him to be a witness against himself. (616, 633)

[78] *Mapp*, 367 U.S. at 646.

[79] *Id.* at 651.

neighborhood, but good enough. The congratulatory notes Clark received from justices who agreed with him are almost creepy in a conspiracy-theory sort of way: "That is a mighty fine opinion you have written," notes super-hyper-liberal William O. Douglas.[80] Justice Brennan writes, "Of course you know I think this is just magnificent and wonderful."[81] This sort of reaction from liberal justices on the court would have made suspicious those conservatives who thought the court was out purposely to change American society in its political image—if they'd been allowed to see them. It even bothered Justice John Harlan, who asked Clark to reconsider "facing the Court, in a case which otherwise should find a ready and noncontroversial solution [the original First Amendment proposal], with the controversial issues that your proposed opinion tenders."[82] In 1983, more than twenty years after *Mapp*, retired Justice Potter Stewart, who opposed Clark's opinion, was still asking: "What provision of the Constitution forbids the judiciary to admit illegally obtained evidence?"[83] The answer is: none in 1961, none in 1983, and none today.

How one reacted to *Mapp* following the announcement depended on one's point of view. The general public reading *Time* magazine must have thought the decision made the world a better place—a brief 277-word article on the court's decisions that June noted the court "reversed a twelve-year-old ruling and eliminated a judicial double standard that had permitted the use of illegally procured evidence in state courts but not in federal courts."[84] What? The inference is that some obscure ruling in 1949 had been in error and the court was simply fixing things up. The writer must have known he could have gotten a bigger reaction from his readers had he mentioned that the court, for the first time in the nation's history, *required states to throw out evidence in state trials* based on how it was obtained, but he apparently chose to make it seem as if the court was merely tidying up some 1949-vintage litter.

Those who actually had to enforce the laws of the states felt differently, with one stating, "The imposition of the exclusionary rule upon the states is the most significant event in criminal law since the adoption of

---

[80] "Memo from Justice Douglas to Justice Clark (April 29, 1961)," *The Papers of Justice Tom C. Clark*, http://utopia.utexas.edu/explore/clark/files/1960-236/case-files/a115-06-01-01-1024.jpg.

[81] "Memo from Justice Brennan to Justice Clark (May 1, 1961)," *The Papers of Justice Tom C. Clark*.

[82] Dorin, "Marshaling Mapp," 401, 426.

[83] Stewart, "The Road to Mapp v. Ohio and Beyond," 1365, 1383.

[84] "Busy End," *Time*, June 30, 1961.

the fourteenth amendment."[85] The author was a young Arlen Specter, later a United States senator, who at the time was an assistant district attorney in Philadelphia.[86] Specter was optimistic, believing the court was "leaving it up to the state to determine the legality of the seizure within broad 'due process' limits."[87] Ha, ha, ha. In fact, the court has nitpicked this issue for the past forty-seven years, forcing states to toss out *anything* that sniffs of illegal seizure and let the criminal go. Two decades after that decision, law enforcers felt the "due process limits" hadn't been broad at all. "Twenty years of rigid application of *Mapp. V. Ohio*, the source of the exclusionary rule in state courts, is enough. It has worked intolerable mischief in the criminal courts,"[88] wrote New York's deputy police commissioner in 1981.

Given the end result, defense attorneys could be expected to champion the exclusionary rule, prosecutors to despise it. But what might judges think? Malcolm Wilkey, a judge who spent more than two decades in the Court of Appeals of the District of Columbia Circuit, certainly no enemy of the Supreme Court, believed that anyone "who ignores the record of experience...has to be in love with the rule itself, not the Fourth Amendment."[89] He lists a full dozen costs to society of the exclusionary rule in damning terms such as, "While only the undeniably guilty benefit from the exclusionary rule, it offers innocent victims neither protection nor remedy,"[90] and thanks to its all-or-nothing effect, "the pickpocket will go free, and so will the murderer, if the officer is found to have exceeded the area of 'reasonableness' in making his search and seizure."[91] For centuries, court rules in England and the United States required that anyone trying to keep evidence *out* of a trial must show good cause for doing so, but backers of the exclusionary rule turn the procedure on its head, demanding that those who want to bring good evidence *in* must prove the need. While backers of the rule claim it exists to deter police misconduct,[92] Judge Wilkey notes "several empirical studies on the effects of the exclusionary rule which

---

[85] Arlen Specter, "Mapp v. Ohio: Pandora's Problems for the Prosecutor," *U. Pa. L. Rev.* 4 (1962), 111.

[86] *Id.* at 4, FNd1.

[87] *Id.* at 8.

[88] Kenneth Conboy, letter to the editor, *New York Times*, October 6, 1961.

[89] Judge Malcolm Richard Wilkey, *Enforcing the Fourth Amendment by Alternatives to the Exclusionary Rule* (Washington, DC: National Legal Center for the Public Interest, 1982), 95 F.R.D. 211, 212.

[90] *Id.* at 218.

[91] *Id.* at 224.

[92] See Mapp v. Ohio, 367 U.S. 643, 660 (1961) (majority opinion stating, "We can no longer permit [the Fourth Amendment] to be revocable on the whim of any police officer...who chooses to suspend its enjoyment").

were made between 1950 and 1971 in five major American cities—Boston, Chicago, Cincinnati, New York, and Washington, D.C. All of the studies but one concluded that the exclusionary remedy was a failure in deterring illegal police conduct."[93]

As hard as it might be to turn around a loaded supertanker, turning around the Supreme Court is even harder. In the fifty years since *Mapp*, decisions have nibbled around the edges of the exclusionary rule—for example, *United States v. Leon*[94] and its "good faith" exception to the rule—but the rule stands. *Mapp v. Ohio* was clearly a power grab by the Warren court, bent on bending America to its view of reality, the typical liberal view that feels sympathy for criminals but not their victims. That is the only explanation that fits Justice Clark's need to produce a Fourth Amendment case from a First Amendment one, and his need to turn a case of Cleveland police misbehavior into manacles for two generations of peace officers and prosecutors. Legal pragmatists pride themselves on making decisions based on their practical outcomes. Thousands of criminal cases have been affected by the exclusionary rule since 1961, but its primary outcome may have been the exclusion of common sense from our criminal justice system.

---

[93] Wilkey, *Enforcing the Fourth Amendment by Alternatives to the Exclusionary Rule*, 95 F.R.D. 211, 227.
[94] 468 U.S. 497 (1984).

CRIMINALS HAVE RIGHTS. STATES? NOT SO MUCH.
GIDEON V. WAINWRIGHT (1963)

I don't object to the idea of states providing attorneys for defendants in serious criminal cases—like so much else in this nation, that's the business of the states themselves. However, I do object to the Supreme Court's *Gideon* decision that *requires* states to provide defense attorneys for defendants who couldn't afford them. It had a laudable legal goal: a leveling of the playing field between prosecution and defense. And Henry Fonda played Gideon in the movie *Gideon's Trumpet*, which means Gideon must have been a great guy, right? But the decision shows how, by 1963, the Warren court had become increasingly arrogant and dismissive of what the states might want, deciding that states should do what *it* wanted simply because it said so.

It also was one of the first "unfunded mandates" that the court and Congress have dumped on states in the past half century, which require states to not only do those things the federal government demands, but also pay for them with no help from Uncle Sam. And it also shows the lie behind the Warren court's opinion of *stare decisis*, the theory that the court should, if at all possible, go along with earlier decisions it made in a matter. In *Gideon*, the court had an identical case from twenty years earlier that it decided to ignore—once again, simply because it wanted to.

As in so many landmark cases, the citizen involved was not as admirable as portrayed in later write-ups. Clarence Gideon was a typical lifelong criminal, one who never did anything serious enough to get headlines, but who stayed in trouble for decades. He spent a year in reform school at age sixteen then received a ten-year sentence for burglary in 1929. As one short biography noted, "He served additional prison stretches at Leavenworth, Kan., for stealing government property; in Missouri for burglary, larceny and escape, and in Texas for theft."[95] Gideon married four times and was an alcoholic and gambler who stole to augment what little he made legally. His children were taken from him by the state of Florida. Doesn't sound much like Henry Fonda, does he? Finally, Gideon was charged with breaking into a poolroom in Florida and stealing change from vending machines. A judge (who apologized for not being able to give Gideon a free lawyer) took a look at his sorry resume after the jury found him guilty and sentenced Gideon to five years in prison, the maximum for the crime. In prison and sober, Gideon began the long appeals process that brought his case to the Supreme Court.

By the time the court heard the case, *Gideon v. Wainwright* had a full twenty-two states as friends of the court that wanted Gideon to win; their attorneys general believed that states *should* provide legal counsel for poor defendants free of charge. Only two states joined with Florida to argue the other side. Instead of assuming those twenty-two were right, the question should be asked: why did those states want to force all the others to do so? There clearly was no constitutional bar to providing counsel, any more than there was a constitutional bar to handing out free tennis rackets to citizens; but why the need to require *other* states to do so? My other concern is the court's use of the term "constitutional right." When did a right go from being something that citizens were allowed to do to something that states are *required to give us?*

The "identical case" I mentioned was one called *Betts v. Brady*[96] from twenty years earlier. And don't take my word for it—here's what Justice Black says in his *Gideon* opinion:

> The facts upon which Betts claimed that he had been
> unconstitutionally denied the right to have counsel appointed
> to assist him are strikingly like the facts upon which Gideon

[95] David Krajicek, "The Clarence Gideon Story," *TruTV,* http://www.trutv.com/library/crime/gangsters_outlaws/cops_others/clarence_gideon/6.html.

[96] Betts v. Brady, 316 U.S. 455 (1942).

here bases his federal constitutional claim...Betts was denied any relief, and, on review, this Court affirmed. [97]

Let me explain this *stare decisis* issue in a way that will bring it home. Let's say you're issued a speeding ticket for driving 79 miles per hour in a 65 miles per hour zone. No problem; you show up in court two weeks later to plead guilty and pay the fine. Sorry, they tell you, the Supreme Court issued a new ruling on the matter and from now on the punishment for speeding will be death by firing squad. Certainly you would want to know *why* the court decided that after decades of allowing people to pay fines, shooting was the new routine.[98] That comprehensive explanation is the sort of thing supposedly required when the court uproots *stare decisis.* But note what Justice Black said in *Gideon* about why *Betts v. Brady* should now be disregarded:

> Since the facts and circumstances of the two cases are so nearly indistinguishable, we think the *Betts v. Brady* holding, if left standing, would require us to reject Gideon's claim that the Constitution guarantees him the assistance of counsel. Upon full reconsideration, we conclude that *Betts v. Brady* should be overruled.[99]

Once again the justices of the Warren court decide to change a long-standing[100] precedent simply because they want to.

The earlier case, on an appeal out of Maryland, took a look at the background of due process of law and noted that the "right to counsel" in the Bill of Rights was not a *guarantee* of counsel, but rather a reversal of English laws of the time that wouldn't even allow a lawyer to appear for a defendant in most cases. "The constitutional provisions to the effect that a defendant should be 'allowed' counsel or should have a right 'to be heard by himself and his counsel,' or that he might be heard by 'either or both,' at his election, were intended to do away with the rules which denied representation...by counsel in criminal prosecutions, *but were not aimed to compel the state to provide counsel for a defendant*"[101] (italics added). The court pointed

---

[97] Gideon v. Wainwright, 372 U.S. 335, 338–9 (1963).

[98] This couldn't happen for myriad reasons, but it gives you an idea of what occurs when the court abruptly changes its mind.

[99] *Gideon*, 372 U.S. at 339.

[100] This precedent had stood for more than 150 years. *Betts* was just the most recent upholding of it.

[101] *Betts,* 316 U.S. at 466.

out—correctly—that the Fifth and Sixth Amendments protected citizens from the federal government, and the Fourteenth protected due process from the states' encroachments; the court also noted that in the cases it had decided requiring states to provide counsel, the states themselves had laws requiring it!

The *Betts* opinion then went through a roundup of state laws in the matter, noting that most all states had constitutional guarantees that tracked the Sixth Amendment, but how they interpreted them varied. Based on their constitutions, three states provided attorneys to indigent defendants; eighteen states' laws required appointment of attorneys in all criminal cases for people who couldn't afford them; six required nothing; a dozen furnished lawyers in felony cases; and eight allowed them in capital (death penalty) and other serious felonies. Virginia had no law of any sort on the issue. But this court was clearly aware that the point of having different states in the union was to have different laws:

> This material demonstrates that, in the great majority of the States, it has been the considered judgment of the people, their representatives, and their courts that appointment of counsel is not a fundamental right, essential to a fair trial...In the light of this evidence, we are unable to say that the concept of due process incorporated in the Fourteenth Amendment obligates the States, whatever may be their own views, to furnish counsel in every such case.[102]

That was in 1942. But the Warren court, around since 1953, had decided *never* to trust the states. As far as these justices were concerned, the Tenth Amendment, which reserved most powers for the states and their citizens, was just polite wording, and it was their job to tell everyone what to do in all cases, all the time. In justifying its demand that all states toe the line, the court's opinion cites *Powell v. Alabama,* the case later made famous as the "Scottsboro Boys" case from 1932. But that wasn't about providing free counsel to defendants unable to afford attorneys—it involved young black men getting cheated out of any sort of fair trial at all. The seven defendants were accused of raping two white women on a train headed across the South, and they were taken off the train and put on trial in Scottsboro, Alabama.

---

[102] *Id.* at 471.

Within a day they had been indicted (all pleaded not guilty), *and six days later they were on trial for their lives.* No wonder the Supreme Court ruling in the case noted, "We hold that defendants were not accorded the right of counsel in any substantial sense. To decide otherwise would simply be to ignore actualities."[103] In other words, this case was about the defendants not receiving their right to counsel as specified in the Sixth Amendment (and in the Alabama Constitution). What the court did thirty-one years later was decide that "right to counsel" meant a free lawyer for almost every criminal defendant. It's sort of like saying the Second Amendment's "right to bear arms" means that states should provide every citizen with a .45 automatic free of charge. Under the Bill of Rights, we all have rights to be free of government interference in a number of ways,[104] but it wasn't until the mid-twentieth century that the Supreme Court decided "rights" meant we were guaranteed *things.* That led to preposterous claims in recent years, such as a "right" to free education, free housing, or free health care, which should lead to the obvious question: at whose expense? Of course, that's the sort of question that legislatures have to worry about, not Supreme Courts acting in place of legislatures. They just hand down a ruling and tell everyone they'd better get in line.

Another key case for the court in *Gideon* was *Palko v. Connecticut* from 1937. In this case, the state took one bite at the apple in a trial and got Palko found guilty of second-degree murder. Not good enough, prosecutors decided, and they filed an appeal on exactly the same case, hoping to get him for first-degree murder. Now if you've watched even a little bit of television over the years, you've heard about the "double jeopardy" section of the Fifth Amendment that prohibits anyone from being tried twice for the same charge. But note what the court said in *Palko*:

> We have said that, in appellant's view, the Fourteenth Amendment is to be taken as embodying the prohibitions of the Fifth. His thesis is even broader. Whatever would be a violation of the original bill of rights (Amendments I to VIII) if done by the federal government is now equally unlawful by force of

---

[103] Powell v. Alabama, 287 U.S. 45, 58 (1932).

[104] Actually, the Bill of Rights is simply meant to keep the federal government off our backs, as discussed shortly, but the court needed extra help to take over state legislatures, too.

the Fourteenth Amendment if done by a state. There is no such general rule.[105]

What? Doesn't everyone know the Fifth Amendment applies to every American? Well, yes, it does, but only as regards the federal government. Even the Supreme Court before Earl Warren didn't have the gonads to claim it involved states as well. Instead they were sidling up to the idea by "incorporating" some of the Bill of Rights through the Fourteenth—the first amendment that *did* apply to the states themselves, since that was the only way to make sure slavery was dead and gone. But note that even Justice Cardozo, a big screaming liberal, had to say that claiming that everything in the Bill of Rights now applied to the states through the Fourteenth was going too far: "There is no such general rule."

So how does the Supreme Court get around to negating what it had spent decades deciding? The way it often does: by first admitting it was correct in all those previous instances—and then changing things anyway! Justice Robert Jackson's opinion notes that on the basis of this historical data, "the Court [in *Betts*] concluded that 'appointment of counsel is not a fundamental right, essential to a fair trial.' It was for this reason the *Betts* Court refused to accept the contention that the Sixth Amendment's guarantee of counsel for indigent federal defendants was extended to or, in the words of that Court, 'made obligatory upon, the States by the Fourteenth Amendment.'"[106] So the previous decision made it very clear. Now the court has to go back, dig up the same precedents, *but come to a different conclusion*. Then the buggy ride begins: "We think the court in *Betts* had ample precedent for acknowledging that those guarantees of the Bill of Rights which are fundamental safeguards of liberty immune from federal abridgment are equally protected against state invasion by the Due Process Clause of the Fourteenth Amendment."[107] Well, maybe they did have ample precedent, but they didn't make that decision. The opinion then goes back to several decisions made before *Betts* and states:

> The fact is that, in deciding as it did—that "appointment of counsel is not a fundamental right, essential to a fair trial"— the Court in *Betts v. Brady* made an abrupt break with its own

---

[105] Palko v. Connecticut, 302 U.S. 319, 324 (1937).

[106] Gideon v. Wainwright, 372 U.S. 335, 340 (1963).

[107] *Id.* at 341.

well-considered precedents. In returning to these old precedents, sounder, we believe, than the new, we but restore constitutional principles established to achieve a fair system of justice.[108]

What the court doesn't bother to mention is that those "old precedents" had nothing to do with requiring that states provide attorneys for defendants in state trials—they were either federal cases or state cases that dealt with fundamental guarantees of law such as *habeas corpus*. In *Gideon*, the Warren court continues its campaign of making the states' constitutions unnecessary by applying the US Constitution to everything the states did. As noted, most states already provided attorneys for defendants unable to afford their own. Now the Supreme Court notes, "From the very beginning, our state and national constitutions and laws have laid great emphasis on procedural and substantive safeguards designed to assure fair trials before impartial tribunals in which every defendant stands equal before the law. This noble ideal cannot be realized if the poor man charged with crime has to face his accusers without a lawyer to assist him."[109] A noble goal, no doubt, but the *Gideon* decision upset the national applecart in three separate ways.

First, it took the Sixth Amendment guarantee of *access to counsel* and made it a guarantee of counsel *paid for by someone else*—certainly not the way the Constitutional Congress meant it to be construed.

Second, in making the Sixth Amendment applicable to all the states through the Fourteenth, the court ignored the Tenth Amendment, which states, "The powers not delegated to the United States by the Constitution, nor prohibited by it to the States, are reserved to the States respectively, or to the people." This amendment was to allow states the freedom to set up their own constitutions and laws. For instance, almost all crimes are crimes because of state laws. Murder is a state-level crime, as was the burglary that Clarence Gideon was convicted of. In making its decision in *Gideon v. Wainwright*, the Supreme Court is saying it trusted the states and their citizens so little that it has to inject federal controls into their legal systems. But if the citizens and the states, which formed the federal government, can't be trusted, what better reason do we have for trusting the federal government itself—especially nine lawyers no one has elected?

---

[108] *Id.* at 343–44.

[109] *Id.* at 344.

Third, allowing the *Gideon* decision simply opens up the states' legal systems to endless tinkering by the Supreme Court. The decision quotes *Powell v. Alabama* by saying that if a defendant is "left without the aid of counsel, he may be put on trial without a proper charge, and convicted upon incompetent evidence, or evidence irrelevant to the issue or otherwise inadmissible. He lacks both the skill and knowledge adequately to prepare his defense, even though he have a perfect one. He requires the guiding hand of counsel at every step in the proceedings against him. Without it, though he be not guilty, he faces the danger of conviction because he does not know how to establish his innocence."[110] Ah, a noble aspiration. But what *is* competent counsel? What if the court decides everyone deserves the level of counsel the richest people can afford, with experts to help choose a jury, experts to counter every one of the prosecution's claims, two or three lawyers at the defendant's table? Once the court has decided that everyone gets a free lawyer, what's to prevent it from saying everyone gets the best of everything all the time? Since the court has tossed away the Constitution and its own precedents, nothing but its own desires are left to restrain it from making all sorts of demands on taxpayers and lower courts. Perhaps all defendants should just be declared innocent and sent home to guarantee that the state didn't step on any of their rights—would the court be happy with that?

After all, the criminal justice system is supposed to find people guilty of committing crimes. As noted in the *Miranda* chapter as well as here, few people ever argue that the defendants in these cases were actually *innocent*—Clarence Gideon was a lifelong criminal, and the chances of his not having broken into that Florida pool hall were glimmeringly small. Over the past half century or so, the Supreme Court has lost sight of the basic decision to be made in court: did the defendant commit the crime or not? Guaranteeing freedom to a person who actually is a criminal is just as much a perversion of justice as convicting the rare person who actually is innocent of the crime with which he's charged, but liberals don't see it that way. As economist Thomas Sowell once wrote, everyone believes people should be assumed innocent until proven guilty. It's just that liberals assume everyone is innocent even *after* they are proven guilty.

---

[110] *Powell,* 287 U.S. at 68–9.

WHY LOOK FOR REASONS WHEN YOU CAN JUST MAKE THIS STUFF UP? *GRISWOLD V. CONNECTICUT* *(1965)*

If you are innocent enough to believe that the Supreme Court decided one day in 1973, based entirely on the evidence in one court case, to require legalized abortion in all fifty states, I congratulate you on your optimism. Sadly, the reality is that the court had been planning the moment for years. There was no precedent for the justices to use in deciding *Roe v. Wade*, so they had to invent one, which they did in *Griswold v. Connecticut*. Absolutely nothing to support its decision in *Roe v. Wade* existed before *Griswold*, but since *Griswold* would not get as much attention as legalization of abortion, the court could do all of its sleight-of-hand there and wait until *Roe* to pull the rabbit fetus out of the hat.[111]

Griswold was a case challenging the availability of contraceptives in the blue-nosed (in those days) state of Connecticut. Before I discuss the case any further, I want to point out what many lawyers know but few "civilians" do: lots of cases in courts are simply conjured up to test a legal ruling. Most of the disability cases against businesses and discrimination cases against renters or home sellers don't actually involve anyone who really wants to

---

[111] Go ahead, kill your kid (excuse me, exercise your "freedom of choice"). But the law allowing you to do so (or not) should be a state law, not a federal government fiat handed down by nine old guys. In fact, state laws did control it in 1973. You could get an abortion in New York but not in Oklahoma. That's why they call it the United *States* of America.

enter a building in a wheelchair or rent an apartment to live in. Instead, the plaintiffs are stalking horses who hope to catch a business making a mistake (innocent or not) and then nail it for many thousands. The plaintiffs and lawyers (who present themselves as good-hearted public-interest attorneys) then split the tens of thousands of dollars the panicked business offers in settlement, usually after some reporter with no legal education discusses the case on the nightly news, believing that it's the real thing.

Griswold was likewise a put-up job, with a couple from the Connecticut Planned Parenthood organization claiming they were not allowed to use contraceptives and the American Civil Liberties Union in on the deal.[112] The truth was that anyone old enough to look over a drugstore counter had been able to buy these things for years; it was just the law that was outmoded (and ignored). But again, this wasn't done for that reason; you have to look at Justice Douglas's opinion to see the real reason. It's in *Griswold* that Douglas lays the foundation for *Roe v. Wade,* finding that fundamental right to privacy that no one else had seen in the Constitution for 178 years. That long a time without discovery in a document as short as our Constitution is pretty good evidence that it wasn't there in the first place, but that never stopped the Warren court. Even for the Warren court, this invention of new rights out of quantum foam was pretty nervy, and the final lineup showed it. Hippie-dippie, hyperliberal tree-hugger William O. Douglas wrote the opinion, but it wasn't even a majority he spoke for. His opinion was followed to the letter only by two other justices. Chief Justice Earl Warren, joined by Justices Arthur Goldberg and William Brennan, filed a concurrence.[113] Then Justice John Harlan wrote his own concurrence, Justice Byron White wrote *his* own concurrence, and Justices Hugo Black and Potter Stewart joined to write the dissent. Got that? Keeping in mind that this case was used as most of the reason for *Roe v. Wade,* it should appall you that only three justices actually approved the opinion *in toto*.

Going through this case is complex, but worth it to understand just how far away from actual jurisprudence the Warren court had gone in twelve

---

[112] "Appellant Griswold is the Executive Director of the Planned Parenthood League of Connecticut." (Griswold v. Connecticut, 381 U.S. 479 [1965]). Can it *be* any clearer than that?

[113] Opinions are what form the case law that people can later use as a precedent; concurrences go along with the main part of the opinion, and those justices, in concurring, back the main push of the decision but disagree with other parts of the opinion. Dissents are by justices who disagree with the opinion and explain exactly why. Often the dissent in a case is better-reasoned than the opinion, mostly because the guy who writes the opinion knows he has the victory in the bag; the dissenter wants to tell history why that guy was wrong and goes to great pains to prove it.

short years. At the start of the opinion, Bill Douglas tries to explain why he and three other justices voted to grant *certiorari* to a case that resulted in only a hundred-dollar fine (that is, they allowed it to be argued before the court). Supreme Court appeal decisions are supposed to apply to big cases that involve fundamental rights—otherwise why waste the time of the high court? In *Griswold*, Douglas might as well have been ruling on whether Maine's nickel-a-can soft drink deposit law was constitutional, with the case brought by a guy who didn't like paying $1.20 deposit on a case of Mountain Dew. After all, it was simply a couple complaining that they hadn't been able to buy contraceptives in one particular instance. Why bother to accept a case like that unless you have a previous undisclosed agenda?

"Coming to the merits," Douglas writes, "we are met with a wide range of questions that implicate the Due Process Clause of the Fourteenth Amendment."[114]

Oh really? Remember that the Due Process Clause in that amendment was passed to keep Southern states from toasting former slaves over barbecue pits and other illegal processes. Even with previous Supreme Court stretching, the law was believed to apply to "due process" that interfered with the basic rights of defendants in serious criminal cases. Hundred-dollar fines were way below that threshold, and Douglas knew it as he tried to cover his butt a few lines later by writing, "We do not sit as a super-legislature to determine the wisdom, need and propriety of laws that touch economic problems, business affairs *or social conditions* [italics mine]. The law, however, operates directly on the intimate relation of husband and wife and their physician's role in one aspect of that relation."[115]

Anyone who runs around claiming that the government should keep its hands off her body as a defense for a national "right to choose" should consider that statement. To allow future generations of Earth-biscuit feminists to complain that the government should stay out of their bodies, Douglas had to claim the federal government *had a right to regulate their bodies that overrode the states' rights to do so, and the Supreme Court could do it without Congress passing a law.* If that doesn't scare you, you snoozed all through high school civics (or went to school after they decided civics should be replaced by eco-enviro-recycling-global-warming indoctrination).

---

[114] Griswold v. Connecticut, 381 U.S. 479, 482 (1965).

[115] *Id.*

But how's Douglas going to justify this? He's going to do it by claiming people have a "fundamental right to privacy" that state legislatures cannot override, and *that* will be based on the First Amendment's Right to Association, which was passed so people could freely get together (in public) to protest government policies and perform other political acts that British kings had often barred. So how does he follow up the statement above? Like this: "The association of people *is not mentioned in the Constitution or the Bill of Rights* [again, my italics but Douglas's exact words]."[116] So he's saying, in effect, "I *am* making this stuff up, and you can't stop me. Watch while I give my liberal buddies the power to tell you what to do without ever getting a legislature to approve it, because we know you wouldn't stand for such legislation."

Justice Douglas then goes on to round up a list of Supreme Court decisions that nibble around the edges of what the Constitution hadn't specified—"the right to educate one's children as one chooses," a right that no doubt existed but had to be specified because states had decided government-run schools should be forced on everyone, and "freedom to associate and privacy in one's associations" out of a case involving the NAACP in Alabama.[117] Now, protecting black Americans from Southern bigots is *exactly* why the Fourteenth Amendment was passed, so ruling that the NAACP could keep its membership rolls private fits right into it. Applying this case to the sale of contraceptives was a big jump, but no problem for Douglas. "In other words," he continues, "the First Amendment has a penumbra where privacy is protected from governmental intrusion."[118] This is the sentence that has angered so many observers over the years. A penumbra of a right? What the hell does *that* mean? It is possible to know what a penumbra *is*—it's the secondary shadow that forms in a solar eclipse where the moon does not completely cover the sun's disk. *But what does that have to do with the United States Constitution?* The framers had created the Bill of Rights so that people, for the first time in history, could know exactly what their rights were, so there would be a sharp line between what the government could control and what was allowed its citizens. Here the Warren court was saying, in essence, "Hey, some of this stuff gets pretty fuzzy. We may decide there are some 'shadow rights' that exist simply because we feel like it, so don't get too secure about the Constitution saying this or that. Just check with us for the last word."

---

[116] *Id.* at 482.

[117] NAACP v. Alabama, 357 U.S. 449 (1958), for those of you playing the home game.

[118] *Griswold*, 381 U.S. at 483.

This went against everything that 178 years of constitutional law stood for, and it was all overthrown for a hundred dollars and a pack of rubbers.

Douglas then goes through a couple more cases that have no bearing on women's bodies or privacy, such as one in which a former member of the Communist Party was allowed to practice law (that must have warmed the hearts of Douglas's liberal buddies).[119] Then he makes the previously fuzzy penumbra talk even fuzzier: "The foregoing cases suggest that specific rights in the Bill of Rights have penumbras, formed by emanations from those guarantees that help give them life and substance."[120]

So let's see: Douglas admits the Bill of Rights lists specific rights the people have that the government cannot override. But these specific rights have hazy sort-of shadows formed by magical intangible and invisible forces that come from those same rights, without which those rights wouldn't exist. So it's actually the "penumbras" that give us those rights, not something as boring as actual words in an actual historic document! From all this, Justice Douglas points to the Fourth Amendment's guarantee against unreasonable search and seizure of evidence in people's houses and the Fifth Amendment's famous right against self-incrimination, and says these two "create a zone of privacy which government may not force him to surrender to his detriment."[121]

Well, that should do it—except Douglas knows it doesn't. He goes back to the secondary-shadow things, saying the justices "have had many controversies over these penumbral rights of 'privacy and repose.'"[122] Later he notes, "We deal with a right of privacy older than the Bill of Rights."[123] Huh? Wasn't the Bill of Rights written to state clearly what our rights were? Then how could something "older than the Bill of Rights" survive as a right, despite the Constitution? Do other formerly accepted rights "older than the Bill of Rights" exist? How about cannibalism? That goes way back. What I'm saying is that once you decide you can use something that *isn't* in the Bill of Rights to decide on what a personal right is, you can do anything you want. And that's just what the Warren court felt it could do.

Was there any voice of reason in *Griswold*? Yeah, but nobody reads that far. Justice Harlan's concurrence clearly warns against deciding that all of

---

[119] Schware v. Board of Bar Examiners of New Mexico, 353 U.S. 232 (1957).

[120] *Griswold,* 381 U.S. at 484.

[121] *Id. at* 485.

[122] *Id.* .

[123] *Id.*

the Bill of Rights can be enforced against the states (remember, it only applied to the federal government when written, and everyone had agreed on that for more than a century) through the "incorporation doctrine" and warns of exactly what has happened in later years by saying that sticking to the "basic values that underlie our society" will "go farther toward keeping most judges from roaming at large in the constitutional field than will the interpolation into the Constitution of an artificial and largely illusory restriction on the content of the Due Process Clause."[124] "Roaming at large" is exactly what the court has been doing since FDR.

Justice White's concurrence has language that seems quaint in today's society: "Rather, the statute [Connecticut's no-contraceptive law] is said to serve the State's policy against all forms of promiscuous or illicit sexual relationships, be they premarital or extramarital, concededly a permissible and legitimate legislative goal."[125]

Justice Hugo Black wrote the dissent in *Griswold* and did a hell of a job. Too bad he and Potter Stewart were outvoted. They slap down Douglas's claim that the First Amendment protects women's bodies by saying, "Speech is one thing; conduct and physical activities are quite another."[126] Black continues by writing, "The Court talks about a constitutional 'right of privacy' as though there were some constitutional provision or provisions forbidding any law ever passed which might abridge the 'privacy' of any individuals. But there is not."[127] Note that, and remember if you can how Robert Bork was booed by the media and Democrats (at the risk of my being redundant) when he said basically the same thing at confirmation hearings for his nomination to the Supreme Court job in 1989, as reported by *The New York Times*:

> The hearings on the nomination of Judge Robert H. Bork to the Supreme Court have spawned a new controversy over a 1965 Supreme Court ruling that struck down a Connecticut law outlawing the use of contraceptives, even by married couples. In the case, Griswold v. Connecticut, the Court ruled that the law violated a constitutional right to privacy.

---

[124] *Griswold*, 381 U.S. at 490.

[125] *Id.* at 491.

[126] *Id.* at 493.

[127] *Id.*

Judge Bork has long maintained that there is no constitutional right to privacy and that, even though the Connecticut law was "nutty," the Court had no business creating such a right. Over the years he has repeatedly criticized the ruling, calling it "improper" and "unprincipled."

But in the hearings this week before the Senate Judiciary Committee, Judge Bork has tried to minimize the significance of the case, calling it just "a test case on an abstract principle."

His comments drew immediate criticism from family planning and civil liberties groups, which called the issue significant and said it prevented many women from having access to contraceptives.

In his testimony, Judge Bork said the case was instigated by some professors at Yale University, not because Connecticut was enforcing the law but "because they like this type of litigation."[128]

Again, this case was never meant to save any real person from improper treatment by government, but rather to get the Supreme Court to do what the people's elected representatives would not. And so it did, after everyone ignored Hugo Black's warning that "surely it has to be admitted that no provision of the Constitution specifically gives such blanket power to courts to exercise such a supervisory veto over the wisdom and value of legislative policies and to hold unconstitutional such laws *that they believe unwise or dangerous*"[129] (italics mine). "I do not believe," Black says a few lines later, "that we are granted power by the Due Process Clause or any other constitutional provision or provisions to measure constitutionality by our belief that legislation is arbitrary, capricious or unreasonable, or accomplishes no justifiable purpose, or is offensive to our own notions of 'civilized standards of conduct'"[130]. Black was saying the court shouldn't enforce

---

[128] Tamar Lewin, "The Bork Hearings; Bork Is Assailed over Remarks on Contraceptive Ruling," *New York Times*, September 19, 1987.

[129] *Griswold*, 381 U.S. at 495.

[130] *Id.*

Eastern liberal standards on the whole country just because it thought it was politically correct.

But of course that is exactly what happened in *Griswold* and hundreds of similar decisions by the Warren court and later. Instead of a nation of fifty states that allow a broad variety of viewpoints of what was right based on their citizens' beliefs—as the Constitution had planned—we got what a few thousand Ivy League grads between Washington and Boston felt was right for us. You shouldn't wonder why so many people in the heartland wanted Earl Warren impeached.

LICENSE TO KILL—AND ROB, RAPE, ETC. *MIRANDA V. ARIZONA (1966)*

The advantage of being a dictator is the ability to ignore what the riffraff think of one's decisions. Just as Marie Antoinette could (reputedly) say, "Let them eat cake" when the common folk of France had no flour for bread, the Warren court could ignore the effect of its decisions on American citizens. After all, the justices lived in a bubble, being paid better than most of their fellow citizens, catered to by the courtiers of Washington, and protected from the effect of their own decisions by legions of police.[131] Why else would a high court issue an edict whose only beneficiaries were criminals who otherwise would do the right thing and admit their crimes, and instead would now be turned loose to commit more crimes on the law-abiding public?

Here's where a few liberals are protesting, saying that this is not the point of the famous *Miranda* decision. Except, what else *is* the reason, since it only protects the guilty? No one ever argues that the people it frees are innocent lambs who only confessed because of all that police pressure; they simply assert that the poor souls must be protected from justice in the same

---

[131] At least in those days. By 2004, the federally ruled District of Columbia was so lawless, thanks in large part to Warren court decisions "expanding the rights of criminal suspects" that Justice David Souter was mugged while on a jog the evening of April 30. It's appropriate, since Souter is one of the biggest liberals on the court, always looking for a reason to turn a criminal loose on the rest of us. And didn't Souter himself "mug" the first President Bush by convincing him he was a conservative before his nomination?

way they argue that foreign terrorists bent on destruction of the United States aren't to be treated as prisoners of war but rather as accused criminals who deserve the same slippery "due process" as American citizens.

While everyone knows the *Miranda* warning, made famous by thousands of police procedural shows on network television for the past forty years, almost no one knows about the case and the criminals that inspired it. The Supreme Court opinion is much less crisp and concise than the warning itself; it runs almost twenty thousand words and is a near thing with its five-to-four vote.[132] Appropriately, it was the head mischief-maker himself, Chief Justice Earl Warren, who wrote the opinion.

While much of his argument is untenable, he begins with the true statement that the cases involved "raise questions which go to the roots of our concepts of American jurisprudence."[133] That's true because the court was reaching into centuries of established common law and ripping it out by its roots. The chief justice was hanging his opinion on the Fifth Amendment's privilege against self-incrimination. Remember that the Bill of Rights was only meant to protect people against the federal government and that it took well over a century before the court decided on its own to apply it to all activities of the states. Then remember that although *Miranda* is aimed only at police forces, the Constitution itself never makes any mention of police at all, reserving that to the states themselves. It's their problem. If you should choose to read the Bill of Rights itself, you would notice that the Fifth Amendment makes no mention whatsoever of police procedure. It does, in one long, compound sentence mention that no one "shall be compelled in any criminal case to be a witness against himself,"[134] the shortest of four guarantees involving criminal cases.

But note that the requirements Earl Warren and four friends cooked up in *Miranda* are things police must say *while arresting* a criminal suspect—not at trial, as the Fifth Amendment had been held to apply for 177 years. Even arguing that the term "case" could apply to pretrial procedure doesn't help, for the Warren court makes *Miranda* apply to the rights of suspects before they are charged with a specific crime, and by definition

---

[132] Which brings to mind the question: why does Congress need a two-thirds vote to change the Constitution, plus the approval of two-thirds of the states, while all the Supreme Court needs is a bare majority? Because, as explained earlier, ruling on the constitutionality of a law isn't in the Constitution—the court simply decided in 1803 to start doing it.

[133] Miranda v. Arizona, 384 U.S. 436, 439 (1966).

[134] U.S. Const. amend. V.

that's a time before there exists a criminal "case" by any stretch of the imagination. Yes, a person has been arrested, but that happens all the time without a case being filed; even the Supreme Court has allowed up to seventy-two hours of jail time before requiring a person be officially charged. Why not make *Miranda* apply at that point? Mostly because constitutional protections already applied from that time, and the Warren court's *raison d'etre* was to expand the purview of the court; here it gives criminals a get-out-of-jail-free card before they are even put in jail, and applies the Fifth Amendment's guarantee against self-incrimination to a time that could extend to months before the actual trial began. To test the logic, ask yourself whether it would have made sense for the Warren court to declare that another clause of the Fifth Amendment—double jeopardy—also took effect at the same time, and rule that a person could not be *arrested* twice for the same offense instead of not being *tried* twice. That may give you an idea of what a stretch *Miranda* was.

They might never have gotten away with it if the media had been diligent in reviewing their logic, but the 1930s brought the acceptance of socialism by American intellectuals. The idea was that, well, the average guy is an idiot anyway, so we who are more intelligent have to make the hard decisions for them, throwing the riffraff some crumbs whenever they get restive. In time, reporters' reaction to this thought pattern became automatic: since the public was stupid, somebody had to make the tough decisions, and since the Congress was elected by that same idiot public, the only people you could trust to be intelligent and disinterested were people who *weren't* elected—bureaucrats and federal judges. And *they* shouldn't be bound by what Congress and the idiot public wanted, but rather by what was fair—which meant whatever they decided was fair.

To show how the media worked hand-in-hand with the Warren court, I've chosen a single report from *Time* magazine, "Concern about Confessions," published in its April 29, 1966, issue. *Time* actually had a conservative viewpoint into the 1950s, but a generation educated by the "parlor pinkos" of the 1930s (socialism burgeoned during the Depression because of perceived failings of capitalism) moved the magazine leftward, and by 1966 the shift was well underway, though the public may not have noticed.

"Concern about Confessions" started out with an agenda. It was a cover story published between the time the *Miranda* case was heard at the end of February 1966 and the decision was announced in June; clearly the idea was either to affect the upcoming ruling or to prepare the public for the big change coming. Of the fifty-eight paragraphs in the piece, only four provide any "balance" to show the anti-*Miranda* view. Much of the piece is a white-wash of the criminals whose cases were used by the Supreme Court, and most of that features little Danny Escobedo, whose case was decided by the court in 1964 and was a precursor to *Miranda,* requiring police to allow criminal suspects to consult a lawyer as soon as serious interrogation began.[135]

The *Time* piece does everything it can to make a scummy little rat, Escobedo, seem like a hero: it describes him as "a Chicago laborer serving 20 years for first-degree murder," of his brother-in-law rather than the more appropriate "Chicago killer serving 20 years for first-degree murder" but that's just the start. *Time* does its best to make Danny seem inoffensive, with descriptions as "a nobody," "5 ft. 5 in., 106 lbs.," and "at his height, Danny hardly seems a threat to any healthy policewoman." His appeals attorney is allowed to say that, at their first meeting, Danny "looked so small and helpless. There was the enormity of the prison, the towering guards, the prison clothes a little too big for him." How could you not feel sorry for a poor kid like that? "In prison," the story rhapsodizes, "Danny wrote poetry, learned plumbing, discovered psychology. He walked out with a high school diploma, dreams of a good job, and hopes of suing the police for a denial of his civil rights." Then, to prepare us for reality, it adds, "Hardly anything has worked out." Poor little Danny. The piece credulously repeats all of Danny's stories about his life as truth: After his release from prison, Danny gets a job at a drug wholesaler, thanks to his new, unmurdered brother-in-law, quits "to find more pay," then is "braced on a street corner by a drug addict who was also a paid police informer. By odd coincidence, the cops swooped down just as the addict shoved a bagful of barbiturates into Danny's hand."

Were readers really expected to believe that little Danny was still an innocent lamb caught in circumstances beyond his control? If so, *Time* tried their patience two paragraphs later. Danny's second brother-in-law, Mitsura Wakita, happened to have a flat tire right after leaving the relatives of his wife, Grace, (Danny's sister, who had been in on the deal to kill husband number one). "As he got out to fix it, another car drew up and hovered nearby. When he opened the door to get back into his car, automatically

---

[135] Escobedo v. Illinois, 378 U.S. 478.

turning on the inside lights, Mits became an easy target and was shot dead." Despite the fact that poor little Danny "loved him like a brother," Escobedo was brought in for questioning by police "immediately."

One wonders how many brothers-in-law Danny would have to kill before *Time* became suspicious that just maybe little Danny was, in some tragic way, connected. Three? Six? Meanwhile, *Time* continues: "Facing trial next month, Danny groans: 'I just hope that great court in Washington makes a new law greater than mine [the original *Escobedo* decision]. Then maybe we'll be left alone.'" Yeah, maybe the court will make sure all killers will be left alone. Of course, rather than waiting for the US Supreme court to go to all that trouble, *Danny should have stopped killing his brothers-in-law,* but hey, he's just little 106-pound Danny Escobedo—what can he do in this big world?

The *Time* cover story also previews the major players in the *Miranda* case, from California, New Jersey, New York, Illinois, and of course, Arizona, whence came Mr. Miranda himself. It's not as if the Warren court pulled these cases out of a hat—*Time* notes that "the Supreme Court sifted 170 confession appeals and accepted five involving six defendants," which should put to bed any thoughts citizens might have that the great "High Court In the Sky" doesn't show any bias. Clearly the court was looking for its best ammunition to put handcuffs on the police instead of suspects, and if what it found was the *best*, police were obviously not as evil a bunch of "pigs" as liberals wanted them to be: of the six defendants, *Time* had to admit that "all but one of the confessions were apparently true and voluntary." Look at that again—what it means is that the people arrested for these crimes actually committed the crimes and freely admitted it later.

So why did the Supreme Court need to make the ruling? No, really— why did they have to make the *Miranda* decision if all but one of the five cases the court handpicked from 170 cases was clearly *not a* case of police malpractice? One hundred sixty-nine to one is a hell of a record for a baseball team or a detective squad. It should be obvious that *Miranda* was chosen and decided because that's what the Warren court wanted to force on the nation—nothing else. Ernesto Miranda himself "talked freely" to police and "did not request counsel." Even more damning, *Time* writes that "both victims identified him in a lineup." Where is the great travesty of justice? Where is the reason Miranda needed to be decided as it was?

There's more. *Time* mentions the story of poor eighteen-year old John Biron, who "admitted mugging an old woman, who later died." What?

Did she die of pneumonia or fall down the stairs? No, the little weasel obviously caused injuries that resulted in her death; ergo, he *murdered* the old lady, a term that *Time* seems unable to employ, perhaps because it would make Biron seem so, well, *guilty.* Luckily, his lawyer "discovered" a police tape that showed how detectives lied to Biron in order to get his confession, promising to send the adult-age defendant to juvenile court. Luckily for Biron and his hard-working attorney, the Minnesota Supreme Court reversed the jury's guilty verdict. Then comes the punch line as *Time* admits, "He was later reconvicted on other evidence the cops already had."

That's the problem with the Warren court and its apologists—where are all the innocent people *Miranda* was supposed to protect? They didn't exist, because if they had, the ACLU and the media liberals would have found them to justify what they wanted. At least *Time* had the class to admit what everyone alive in the 1960s knew, that we had "a crime rate rising five times faster than the rate of population growth." And the Warren court felt that *criminals* were under attack?

Miranda was actually a compilation of five felony cases from several states (Arizona, New Jersey, Illinois, California, and New York) that supposedly raised the same questions. In his opinion, Chief Justice Warren employs the tools already well honed by his court: use a few citations of cases before there was a Bill of Rights, and then jump straight to the Warren court's own previous decisions, ignoring the great majority of cases that sweep from the adoption of the Constitution to the 1960s. Likewise, misdirection was a favorite of the court. Warren notes several cases that involved near-torture of suspects[136] and uses that as a basis not to rule against torture or maltreatment by police, but rather to enforce his personal views of fairness by making the work of police far more difficult.

Warren begins with the Star Chamber Oath of 1637,[137] which "would have bound {a suspect} to answer all questions posed to him on any subject." Well, yeah, we'll admit it was unfair, and life in 1637 was tough; that was pretty much the reason for the Bill of Rights, which dealt with the problem *150 years later.* Warren jumps over this little matter and quotes

---

[136] Warren cites Wan v. United States, 266 U.S. 1 (1924), a truly awful case of constant questioning of a man bedridden with spastic colitis over a period of ten days. But its ruling that "a confession obtained by compulsion must be excluded" had been made forty-two years earlier. *Miranda* did nothing to extend it; instead it gave criminals a chance to walk free after even a voluntary confession if police failed to perfectly express "magic words" required by the court.

[137] *Miranda,* 384 U.S. at 459.

Boyd v. United States from 1886 that "illegitimate and unconstitutional practices get their first footing…by silent approaches and slight deviations from legal modes of procedure."[138] *Boyd* was a perfect, on-point case that related closely enough to *Miranda* to be used as support for Warren's opinion—well, except that it was a civil case, not a criminal case; it dealt with taxes owed instead of a murder. It involved thirty-five cases of plate glass imported into the United States, though the evidence involved wasn't even about the thirty-five cases of plate glass, but about twenty-nine other cases brought in earlier that the district attorney wanted a receipt for to show the quality of the glass in question. Other than that, it was perfect (and if it were still followed in tax law, the IRS couldn't get enough evidence on any of us to enforce income taxes). So all Warren was using was a quote from the case to justify his imposition of an unprecedented rule that, rather than deal with the Fourth Amendment's guarantee against search and seizure as *Boyd* did, was supposedly built on the Fifth Amendment's guarantee against testifying against oneself (which Warren continually misinterpreted to guarantee against self-incrimination at any time—a quite different matter).

Later the chief justice quotes another case that claimed to guarantee each citizen "a right to a private enclave where he may lead a private life. That right is the hallmark of our democracy."[139] Once again he quotes the Fourth Amendment to buttress his view of the Fifth, because if he had found anything to uphold the Fifth, he would have used it. The Fourth Amendment is a guarantee against unreasonable search and seizure in one's home or private effects, while the Fifth involves testifying against oneself. Now consider the *Miranda* case. Police were questioning suspects, not grabbing stuff hidden under their mattresses, but Warren acted like a guy in a bar fight—grab whatever weapon you can find and use it, whether it makes sense or not.

Then, as was typical of the Warren court, the chief justice cites a case from his own court dealing with a state investigation of gambling that led a commission to declare a witness in contempt because of his refusal to answer questions, something any court can do to a witness any time the witness refuses to testify. (Since the case is not aimed at the witnesses, their testimony is not against themselves under the Fifth Amendment.)[140]

---

[138] 116 U.S. 616, 635 (1886), if looking this stuff up is your idea of a good time.

[139] United States v. Grunewald, 233 F.2d 556, 579, 581–82.

[140] Malloy v. Hogan, 378 U.S. 1 (1964).

Then Warren mentions another of his own court's decisions from the same year,[141] writing, "We hold only that when the process shifts from investigatory to accusatory—when its focus is on the accused and its purpose is to elicit a confession—our adversary system begins to operate, and, under the circumstances here, the accused must be permitted to consult with his lawyer." Once again, the Warren court uses its own earlier decisions to justify yet another extension of its view of the Constitution. First is a rule that the suspect be allowed to consult a lawyer starting at some vague undefined point in an investigation; then comes the rule in *Miranda* that police must tell him or her all this before even beginning questioning. If my complaint seems wacky and neoconservative, allow me to introduce this statement:

> At the very least the Court holds that once the accused becomes a suspect and, presumably, is arrested, any admission made to the police thereafter is inadmissible in evidence unless the accused has waived his right to counsel. The decision is thus another major step in the direction of the goal which the Court seemingly has in mind—*to bar from evidence all admissions obtained from an individual suspected of crime*, whether involuntarily made or not[142] [italics added].

That wasn't made by some whacked-out DA drunk on power, but rather in the dissent to a difficult five-to-four case—the same *Escobedo v. Illinois*—and the dissent was written by Justice Byron White, joined by Tom Clark and Potter Stewart, hardly Scalia-style conservatives. Even these liberals were appalled by the restriction on police power the court was putting into place, and they also knew that the court had an agenda in mind, something the Supreme Court is not supposed to have. Each case supposedly stands on its own and wasn't used as part of a partisan campaign to change the nation, but *Escobedo* and *Miranda* clearly were.

After announcing the list that would later become known as the *Miranda* warning, Chief Justice Warren states, "In announcing these principles, we are not unmindful of the burdens law enforcement officials must bear, often under trying circumstances."[143] Meaning, of course, that he's "not unmindful" of their problems, he just doesn't give a rat's ass about them. "The limits," he

---

[141] Escobedo v. Illinois, 378 U.S. 478 (1964).

[142] *Id.* at 495.

[143] *Miranda*, 384 U.S. at 481.

continues, "should not constitute an undue interference with a proper system of law enforcement." Except that they did exactly that, as history has proved. Let's look at the government's own *Statistical Abstract of the United States* for 1963, which innocently says that "law enforcement is for the most part a function of State and local officers and agencies. The US Constitution reserves general police powers to the States."[144] Of course, the Warren court had no interest in doing what the Constitution required; it wanted the federal government involved in law enforcement no matter what. The abstract for 1963 lists crime from 1961, showing 8,600 murders in the entire United states that year and 91,600 robberies. Sounds scary, but it's nothing, pal. After *Escobedo, Miranda,* and other Warren court actions aimed at making America safe for criminals, the 1973 abstract points out the bad news. In the decade from 1960 to 1970, the country's murder total had jumped 60 percent, rape 90 percent, robbery an astounding 186 percent, and property crimes (burglary and theft) up 113 percent.[145] The good news: suicides had dropped between 1965 and 1970, probably because so many of the poor devils were being murdered first.

After an impossibly long and complex opinion that runs sixty-three pages, its pure length showing the reason why these five cases should never have been slammed together, the dissents begin, written by the three justices who objected to *Escobedo,* joined by Justice Harlan. Justice Tom Clark, likely the most liberal on the court next to William O. Douglas, says the *Miranda* opinion "goes too far on too little"[146] and criticizes the chief justice for extensively quoting "police manuals" as justification for the new rules, instead of actual cases involving actual mistreatment of suspects, and saying that even worse, "not one is shown by the record here to be the official manual of any police department, much less in universal use in crime detection."[147] So this supporting evidence for *Miranda* didn't even come from police manuals being used at the time.

"Moreover," Clark continues, "the examples of police brutality mentioned by the court are rare exceptions to thousands of cases that appear every year in the law reports."[148] If the court is worried about these exceptions, Clark is saying, why not make a rule applying to *the exceptions* rather

---

[144] *Statistical Abstract of the United States: 1963* (Washington, DC: US Census Bureau, 1963), 55.

[145] *Statistical Abstract of the United States: 1973* (Washington, DC: US Census Bureau, 1973), 56. Note that these are crime rates, which means they are adjusted for population growth, so the fact that many baby boomers had come of age in the '60s doesn't affect the matter.

[146] *Miranda*, 384 U.S. at 499.

[147] *Id.*

[148] *Id.* at 499–500.

than a complex procedural requirement to every single criminal case, the slightest infraction of which would turn a likely guilty criminal out on the streets on a free pass? Since no one knows the effect of this, Clark states, "I would be more restrained less we go too far too fast," adding that "such a strict constitutional specific inserted at the nerve center of crime detection may well kill the patient."[149] Which it did. Again, Clark was no conservative—he made his liberal bones writing the *Mapp* decision that threw out evidence unless police were ever-so-careful in guaranteeing everyone's rights in gathering it, and his son, Ramsay Clark, is as far left as any person ever named attorney general of the United States (although we should thank him for one thing—when LBJ named the younger Clark to the job, his dad stepped down from the high court).

The dissent of the other three justices was written by John Harlan, who called the *Miranda* decision "poor constitutional law [that] entails harmful consequences for the country at large. How serious these consequences may prove to be, only time will tell."[150] Once again, a dissent to the Warren court's decisions was much closer to the truth than the (bare) majority.

Also typically, the case that led to an overhaul of criminal law had little to do with the resulting decision. Ernesto Miranda, after whom the warning was named, was arrested for rape in Phoenix on March 13, 1963, and taken to a police station where the rape victim identified him. He confessed after two hours of questioning, certainly not a long time in a felony case; there was no hint of torture or threats on the part of the two police officers who did the interrogating, and they emerged from the session with a confession by Miranda clearly stating he had made it voluntarily. Their sin, as police officers, was simply that they did not tell Miranda he had the right to have an attorney present. Even the Supreme Court of Arizona, when apprised of the oversight, said Miranda had never asked for an attorney and upheld the twenty-year convictions for kidnapping and rape.

The whole situation had a certain poetic justice. Seven years after the Supreme Court decision, Ernesto Miranda was murdered in a fight. The suspect was never taken to trial because he invoked his *Miranda* rights at interrogation, and his attorney told him to clam up. *Time* magazine did not bother to report that little item.

---

[149] *Id.* at 500–01.

[150] *Id.* at 504.

HOW THE SUPREME COURT WRECKED PUBLIC SCHOOLS TINKER V. DES MOINES SCHOOL DISTRICT (1969)

The ACLU and its pals are constantly mewling about civil rights for everyone—children, prisoners, criminal suspects, foreign terrorists—everyone but fetuses and taxpayers. But once they and their minions have successfully convinced the Supreme Court to institute new "rights" for some group, they ignore the damage done by their victory. *Miranda* led to a huge increase in crime nationwide; nowadays, terrorists clearly view lawsuits over Guantanamo detainees as helpful.

Likewise, suits brought in the past forty years to give students "rights" have made it almost impossible to run a public school in a way that allows students who want to learn to do so. This is not only because of the rules the court instituted, but also because of the huge expense of defending against lawsuits brought against school districts on ridiculous grounds. The ACLU and its ilk have no problem collecting cash from hundreds of thousands of limousine liberals and concentrating them on a single school district that the Supreme Court will use to make a ruling that affects *every school in America*. But the cost of fighting the suit falls only on the taxpayers in that one school district. An administrator or school board member who urges an appeal against even the most frivolous suit will be viewed as irresponsible and possibly plain nuts. That's why schools often fold to pre-posterous demands that make it harder for real students to learn, while the kids whose parents have "grievances" and want to vent their political views get the attention and freedom.

So it was with *Tinker*. It's clear that the students involved were nothing more than stalking-horses for their parents' political values. Lead plaintiff John Tinker was fifteen years old and his sister was a thirteen-year-old in junior high, barely old enough to have outgrown Santa Claus. The other plaintiff, Christopher Eckhardt, was all of sixteen.

The opinion in the case starts off by saying that "a group of adults and students" opposed to the war in Vietnam held a meeting at the Eckhardt home. That's true as far as it goes; what it doesn't note is that the parents of all three kids were basically full-time antiwar stooges for the American Friends Service Committee and the Women's International League for Peace and Freedom. The WILPF still exists, and years after the Vietnam War, is still in favor of anything that damages America or makes it or Israel look bad (go to their website and check it out at http://www.wilpf.org). The Tinker kids' dad was receiving full-time pay from the American Friends Service Committee; clearly he had a lot to gain from turning his kids into media darlings. Instead of pointing this out (although Justice Black notes it in his dissent), Abe Fortas's opinion makes it appear as if these kids were struck by good old American First Amendment fervor on their own and decided to wear black armbands to school to protest the war. Why, what could be so bad about that?

A lot. Consider what the average high school administrator faced before the Supreme Court screwed things up. Even then, it was a near thing every day that anyone got any education: from three hundred to twelve hundred students, all going through adolescence, none particularly interested in the subjects at hand, tempted by drugs, alcohol, sex, and television (at least the Internet hadn't been invented yet). It was a struggle every day to keep things from boiling over between the jocks, nerds, stoners, and real gang members. Then along comes the Supreme Court to tell them there's just *one more thing* they have to allow, which is for any student to do anything they want to piss off every other student there. Great.

The court's lack of caring about how the world really works and whether anyone actually gets an education in public school is painfully obvious in the opinion. Justice Fortas points out the District Court actually was foolish enough to uphold the school administration "on the ground that it was reasonable in order to prevent disturbance of discipline." But the high court, apparently none of whom ever had teenagers, instead went along with the Fifth Circuit's "holding in a similar case that the wearing of armbands cannot be prohibited unless it 'materially and substantially interfere[s] with the requirements of appropriate discipline in the operation of the school.'" Nice try, but Iowa is in the Eighth Circuit, not the Fifth, which means that legally, Fortas might as well have been quoting Charles Dickens for support.

Then he says, "The wearing of an armband for the purpose of expressing certain views is the type of symbolic act that is within the Free Speech Clause of the First Amendment," and cites four cases to back it up. However, none of them have anything to do with schools, which is totally the point of *Tinker*. One allowed members of the Young Communist League to fly a red flag at its summer camp in the 1930s, another involved union organizers, the third was over black demonstrators at a segregated public library, and the fourth was a similar antisegregation demonstration at a state capitol. None of these had minors as defendants, and none of them dealt with institutions where attendance is legally compulsory and discipline crucial.

Fortas claimed that "it can hardly be argued that either students or teachers shed their constitutional rights to freedom of speech or expression at the schoolhouse gate." But it certainly *can* be argued, since the students were some years away from being adults (it was twenty-one in those days) and the teachers were at least under the same strictures that can be enforced on any employees at any workplace. Where would Fortas have allowed full First Amendment rights: in the third grade, in kindergarten? The whole idea of an arbitrary age for majority is that, restrictive as it might be to some well-spoken youngsters, it at least creates a line of demarcation. At that age, you get full constitutional rights; before then, you get something less. Instead, the court chose *Tinker* to hand out rights willy-nilly according to a schedule only known to itself, leaving school districts around the country to guess. The opinion made it clear when it said First Amendment rights are to be "applied in light of the special characteristics of the school environment." Which would be...? If, as the court ruled, students are allowed to wear armbands if the action doesn't "materially and substantially interfere" with school discipline, who decides what is enough interference? Only the Supreme Court—the level of which is reached only after millions of dollars in legal bills (and only if four justices decide they want the case). No sane school board would choose that path; it's better just to give in on any challenged act of discipline and let the little bastards do whatever they want.

At the time, Fortas was careful to say the armband case "does not relate to regulation of the length of skirts or the type of clothing, to hair style or deportment." But why not? Why would green hair or a Mohawk "materially and substantially interfere" with school discipline? Why would wearing a barely butt-length miniskirt interfere with discipline, as long as the girl acted primly while at school? It's the sort of hair-splitting that led to the *Tinker* decision; might as well apply it everywhere while you've got the chance.

The vote was seven to two in favor of the Tinkers, but two of those judges made it clear they didn't approve of everything Fortas said. Potter Stewart wrote, "I cannot share the Court's uncritical assumption that, school discipline aside, the First Amendment rights of children are coextensive with those of adults. Indeed, I had thought the Court decided otherwise just last Term in *Ginsberg v. New York.*"[151] And why would the rights of children be "coextensive" with that of adults? Allowing them the same rights destroys the entire concept of children—that these are adults in the process of being formed, but still not adults. If children are assumed to have the same ability to make rational First Amendment decisions as adults, why not assume they have the same ability to make informed decisions about sex and lower the age of consent to, say, eleven or seven years? Why not let five-year-olds vote so Justin Bieber or the latest tween idol can be president?

Ginsberg v. New York had indeed been decided just a year before. In it the court ruled, "It is not constitutionally impermissible for New York... to accord minors under 17 years of age a more restricted right than that assured to adults"[152] when it comes to "girlie" magazines (yep, that's what the Supreme Court called 'em). The case involved a sixteen-year old boy who'd bought a magazine that was not considered obscene for adults (remember those days when states could decide what was obscene?) but was restricted to those seventeen and older. Justice Brennan's opinion stated, "It is cardinal with us that the custody, care and nurture of the child reside first in the parents, whose primary function and freedom include preparation for obligations the state can neither supply nor hinder." Certainly if parents didn't want their kids to see sexually oriented magazines and had the power to forbid it, the court should have thought the next year that parents might

---

[151] Tinker v. Des Moines Sch. Dist., 393 U.S. 503, 515 (1969).

[152] Ginsberg v. New York, 390 U.S. 629 (1968).

not want the controversies of the outside world brought into school and shoved in their children's faces, but it wasn't to be. Is there any wonder that learning in public schools has fallen off since the 1960s?

Clarence Thomas, nemesis of liberals who believe blacks should be Democrats or be quiet, commented on *Tinker* in a later case[153] in which the court limited, somewhat, its decision that students can disrupt school activities. Thomas wrote a concurrence[154] "to state my view that the standard set forth in *Tinker v. Des Moines Independent Community School Dist.* is without basis in the Constitution." In *Morse v. Frederick,* the court backed a principal who suspended a student for unfurling a banner reading "Bong Hits 4 Jesus"[155] at a school activity, which Thomas noted was "another exception" to *Tinker*, "but we neither overrule it nor offer an explanation of when it operates and when it does not." So *Tinker* continues to be the rule, creating the opportunity for endless mischief in schools by students and the ACLU, all at the expense of actual learning.

In the dissent to *Tinker*, Hugo Black predicted what has happened since then: "The Court's holding in this case ushers in what I deem to be an entirely new era in which the power to control pupils by the elected 'officials of state-supported public schools…' in the United States is in ultimate effect transferred to the Supreme Court."[156] And so it was. The outcome has been what occurs when there's a distant parent who only gives a child attention when some outrage happens—the court allows almost anything to go on in public schools and blames the other parent, the now-powerless administrators, when something bad takes place. Black said that, despite the majority's claim that the wearing of armbands by a few students did not disrupt classwork, he felt the whole uproar certainly "diverted" the thoughts of the other children. Then Black made another keen prediction:

> And I repeat that, if the time has come when pupils of state-supported schools, kindergartens, grammar schools, or high schools, can defy and flout orders of school officials to keep their minds on their own schoolwork, *it is the beginning of a*

---

[153] Morse v. Frederick, 551 U.S. 393 (2007).

[154] A concurrence is written by a justice who agrees enough with the majority opinion to vote for it but wants to express some disagreement with it.

[155] In its own way the poster was a masterpiece of conciseness, managing to be pro-drug use and insulting to both good grammar and Christianity in just four words.

[156] *Tinker*, 393 U.S. at 515.

new revolutionary era of permissiveness in this country fostered by the judiciary[157](italics added).

That was, of course, exactly what happened. There's a direct line from *Tinker* to the disaster public schools are today, with their dropouts, violence, pregnancies, tattoos, and all. And that line goes right through the US Supreme Court.

---

[157] *Id.* at 503, 518 .

WHEN WELFARE BECAME A CAREER CHOICE
GOLDBERG V. KELLY (1970)

In 1970, some people may have thought that welfare payments were for people who had no other choice and just needed a bit of cash to get back on their feet. If you don't know better than that today, you are seriously deluding yourself. Welfare and other such payments (WIC, "job training," food stamps, etc.) are either a base salary given so you have time to plan your next crime or a reward for bringing more half-parented offspring into the world.

How did things get so bad? Once again, you can thank the Supreme Court. While *Goldberg v. Kelly* was actually decided after Earl Warren left the court, his pals were still hard at work, easily outvoting the new, (somewhat) more conservative chief justice, Warren Burger, leaving the new boss nothing to do but write a sputtering dissent. After almost two decades of running the country, the justices had become so arrogant about their power that they hardly did more than nod toward precedent.

Justice Brennan's opinion notes, "the constitutional issue to be decided, therefore, is a narrow one whether the Due Process Clause requires that the [welfare] recipient be afforded an evidentiary hearing before the termination of benefits."[158] Well, sort of. In fact, the state of New York had no requirement whatsoever for a hearing for welfare recipients until the case

---

[158] Goldberg v. Kelly, 397 U.S. 254 (1970).

arose. The logic behind welfare payments, until the Warren court got its hands on it, was the rational concept that welfare is money *given* to someone for doing nothing; ergo, it is charity. A person accepting charity has no further right to it—imagine the bum on the corner demanding five bucks from you every day because you gave that much to him once in a moment of wet-eyed weakness. But of course, slam-dunking camels through eyes of needles is nothing for bureaucrats—the more people you can get on welfare, the more people there are dependent on state employees, the more government jobs and raises for them.

That "hearing" required by the state came once the case was filed claiming that welfare recipients were being cheated by not getting hearings when their benefits were terminated. The state's politicians came up with a simple hearing requirement, hoping that throwing a bone to a slavering Cujo could arrest his appetite. Fat chance. So, having given in on the key issue, all the Supreme Court had to do was tap a few nails into the coffin. That's why Brennan said his decision was on "narrow" grounds. The monkey wrench he was throwing was the term "evidentiary hearing." A pretermination hearing may be a straightforward thing involving a couple of guys in short-sleeved dress shirts and clip-on ties, but an *evidentiary* hearing is basically a trial.

To give you an idea of what that means, consider that fewer than five percent of all lawsuits and criminal cases filed in this country actually end up in a courtroom, for the simple reason that a trial and preparation for it is a big, expensive, time-consuming pain in the ass. Imagine having one for every bum getting (in those days) a hundred bucks a month who didn't deserve to receive those hundred bucks. Add that to the fact that bureaucrats only benefit from larger welfare rolls, and you can see why we ended up with the mess we have today.

But hey, the Supreme Court wouldn't make a decision like that unless it had precedent, right? Somewhere in the Constitution there must be *something* that guarantees welfare recipients a near-trial before losing their cash cow, right? Well, the opinion does note that "to cut off a welfare recipient in the face of...'brutal need' without a prior hearing of some sort is unconscionable."[159] But that's not in the Constitution—it's from the opinion of a lower federal court in the same case. That's sort of like Dad coming home and having Mom tell him she let Billy set fire to the cat because his

---

[159] *Id.* at 256 (quoting Kelly v. Wyman, 294 F. Supp. 893, 899, 900 (1968).

older sister said it would be all right. The *Federal Rules of Evidence* doesn't allow an attorney to "bootstrap" a witness by calling on someone to say what a great, trustworthy guy he is after the witness has claimed he is a great, trustworthy guy.[160] But here Brennan does the same thing without batting an eye.

As Brennan goes on, it's obvious that he is sailing in shallow waters indeed. In an opinion, you should use your big guns first—set out your best basis for argument early on. For instance, if the matter is mentioned in the Constitution, put it right there, then go down the line of Supreme Court cases dealing with the issue from 1800 on down. But of the first ten cases Brennan cites, *nine* were decided by the Warren court. The other was a case decided just two years before Earl Warren got his position. Legally, this is the equivalent of Mom telling Billy to do something "because I said so." Brennan's foundation for this important constitutional decision wasn't the Constitution, the Congress, or even the Supreme Court of any but the one he sat on. Why must welfare recipients get trial-like termination hearings? Because Justice Brennan said so. Nyaah.

The Warren court treated the concept of due process in much the same way, making it mean whatever they wanted it to mean at any given time. Alexander Hamilton, who was around at the time the Bill of Rights was passed, said that "the words 'due process' have a precise technical import and are only applicable to the process and proceedings of the courts of justice; they can never be referred to an act of the legislature."[161] The Warren court was hardly Hamiltonian; it used due process as a club to smack any number of square pegs into round holes; here they were requiring trial-like procedures in a situation where no one was accused or sued. The due-process concept itself shows the overreaching of the Supreme Court in the past seventy years, since it appears in two places in the Constitution: the Fifth Amendment and the Fourteenth. It is generally agreed that the Fifth Amendment, like all of the first ten, is a restriction on what the federal government can do, while the Fourteenth is a Reconstruction amendment

---

[160] Federal rule of evidence 608(a)(2): "Evidence of truthful character is admissible only after the character of the witness for truthfulness has been attacked by opinion or reputation evidence or otherwise." In other words, you can try to build your guy up only after he's been torn down; "bootstrapping," trying to build upon a foundation your witness has provided with another one in his favor, is a no-no.

[161] Alexander Hamilton, "Remarks on an Act for Regulating Elections," New York Assembly, February 6, 1787, in *Papers of Alexander Hamilton,* edited by Harold Syrett (New York: Columbia University Press, 1977) 34, 35 (quoted in *Black's Law Dictionary, Eighth Edition,* edited by Bryan A. Garner [Eagan, MN: Thomson Reuters Westlaw, 2004] 539).

passed in 1866 aimed at helping freed slaves get all the rights due them ("Nor shall any State deprive any person of life, liberty, or property, without due process of law; nor deny to any person within its jurisdiction the equal protection of the laws."). The Fourteenth was the first amendment applied to states because the post-Civil War Congress couldn't figure out any other way to assure reasonable treatment of former slaves.

Now here's where the court and its apologists get cute. The Fourteenth applies due process to the states, the Fifth applies it to the federal government. But the court, even before Earl Warren, started saying the Fourteenth allows them to apply earlier amendments written for the federal government to the states. This "incorporation doctrine" means that the First, Fourth, Sixth, and Ninth Amendments are required to be observed by the states, even without federal involvement.

Two questions: if that's true, why didn't the backers of the Fourteenth Amendment mention it at the time and perhaps make it clear in the amendment itself?[162] And if the Fourteenth "incorporates" the Bill of Rights for the states, why doesn't it incorporate *all* of the Bill of Rights amendments? And if *that's* true, why is there need for a *second* due process clause in the Fourteenth Amendment to the Constitution? Clearly the sponsors of the Fourteenth Amendment were sure that the Fifth did *not* apply to the states—hence the need for the second due process clause in what was the *only* amendment meant to apply directly to citizens of the various states. Knowing that, you could ask why should that same Fourteenth Amendment be used to "incorporate" the earlier ones?

But you can see why, in claiming that this "incorporation" was intended, the Supreme Court has yet to include the Fifth Amendment; it would be too embarrassing by far to explain—what is the effect of one due process clause multiplied by another? Why would anyone plan to use the Fourteenth Amendment to incorporate the earlier amendments for the states if they put a due process clause in it, knowing one already existed in the Fifth? This is where liberals put their fingers in their ears, stomp the floor, and yell "LA-LA-LA-LA" so they don't have to hear a very clear question that puts the lie to everything they want—that is, federal control of everything the states do.

But if the Constitution was ever meant to control much of what the states could do, why even bother to call it the United *States* of America?

---

[162] There have been attempts to claim the backers did do this, but available quotes are limited to what one sponsor said *after* the amendment was passed.

Why not just call it Fredonia, Liberteria, or something of the sort? The original idea was to let the states do what they wanted, with the federal government simply filling in the cracks between them. But admitting that would not give liberals what they wanted—one-stop shopping at the Supreme Court, in which a single decision would control all fifty states. The ACLU knew it couldn't go to all fifty states and get them to agree to the same laws, but it could focus all its effort on just nine (better yet, just five) men and succeed.

As I said, the state of New York made *Goldberg* easy on Justice Brennan by tossing in that last-minute termination hearing procedure. Because of that, Brennan simply noted that "appellant does not contend that procedural due process is not applicable to the termination of welfare benefits,"[163] and goes on to claim that welfare is a "statutory entitlement" and therefore the challenge "cannot be answered by an argument that public assistance benefits are 'a privilege' and not a 'right.'"[164] As most three-card monte dealers and other grifters know, the trick is to make the important thing seem unimportant while putting forth a lot of effort on something unimportant. This draws your opponent's attention away from the action that really cheats him. Turning welfare into a "right" is itself a complete refutation of the Constitution by forcing productive members of our society into indentured servitude for those who don't want to produce; no wonder Brennan wanted to get the dirty work over quickly. *Goldberg* was what started America down the path to welfare queens and four generations of families never even thinking of working for a living. After *Goldberg*, saying welfare was meant to be temporary and only for folks who couldn't support themselves otherwise was like saying Al Capone went into business just to provide medicinal alcohol for sick people.

When Brennan actually did reach beyond the Warren era for a case to support him, he didn't hesitate to misrepresent it in a way more favorable to his cause. After graciously saying that state welfare boards didn't have to allow "a complete record and a comprehensive opinion"[165] which would have meant a real judge *and* a court reporter, Brennan then quotes the high-sounding phrase, "the fundamental requisite of due process of law is the opportunity to be heard."[166] Brennan figured most people wouldn't bother

---

[163] *Goldberg,* 397 U.S. at 261.

[164] *Id.*

[165] *Id.* at 262.

[166] *Id.* at 262 (quoting Grannis v. Ordean, 284 U.S. 385, 394 [1914]).

to look at the case the quote came from and would be overwhelmed by the lofty prose. In fact, the case, dating from before World War One, dealt with a *real* due process matter—a man whose name was misspelled by the people suing him over a piece of land in Minnesota was thus not properly served, and so he lost the case because he didn't know he was being sued. This was actual due process in an actual case in a real court, and had nothing to do with made-up rights in a sort-of trial/hearing in a bureaucrat's conference room.

So what would I claim in lieu of Brennan's argument? That welfare is indeed a privilege and probably one that shouldn't be handed out. What would replace it? Charity. Those who claim charity could not possibly cover all the people currently on the welfare rolls are missing the point; all those people currently on welfare *shouldn't be there*; the few who are actually incapable of caring for themselves could easily be cared for by private charity. Saying charity removes their "dignity" is also a fatuous argument; how much "dignity" should we allow people who are trying to enforce their unjust claim to money the rest of us have worked for? Besides, the loss of dignity is what welfare payments have caused, not the other way around. We have taken away the legitimacy of hard work and self-respect and replaced it with dependence and *il*legitimacy.

WHY SCHOOL PRAYER DIDN'T HAVE A PRAYER
ENGEL V. VITALE (1962)

The issue of prayer in public schools in this country carries almost as much bad feeling as the issue of abortion. Before I explain how the Warren court found its way to an antireligious stance so strong that major cities in our country would have to be renamed if it were actually enforced,[167] let me first say how I feel about prayer in public schools. I heartily oppose it, but not for the reasons you may think. I oppose it because I think government-owned schooling is one of the worst ideas ever inflicted on this country. Why should we turn our children over to what amounts to liberal indoctrination camps at the age of five? If nothing else, it should be clear that government schools are incompetent because of a combination of factors, from bureaucracy and laziness to unions and political correctness. And if they aren't, why do political candidates and presidents[168] who tell us how important government schools are choose to send their own kids to private schools?

To explain, think about what life would be like if the government had decided that:

---

[167] San Francisco, San Antonio, and St. Louis are named after saints of the Roman Catholic Church. The court has ruled that similar connections between religion and governments are unconstitutional "establishment" of religion—e.g., crosses or crèches used as Christmas decorations.

[168] Bill Clinton and Barack Obama both strongly supported public school unions while sending their own children to expensive private schools. At least Jimmy Carter walked the walk.

a. Every American needed good, healthy food.
b. Private farmers and stores could not be trusted to deliver this food in the proper amounts in the proper locations.
c. Some people were getting wealthy providing these necessities, which must mean the customers were being cheated.
d. Since some people could not afford any of these items they wished, all must be provided to everyone by the government free of charge.

I think you know what would happen—under government control, McDonald's would take twelve hours to deliver a hamburger, it would cost fifteen dollars, and it would never have tomatoes. And you could complain all you wanted and no one would do a damn thing, just as it is today with public highways and government schools.

But on to the main subject: the Warren court's hatred for religion, which was actually the hatred of religion by the American Civil Liberties Union, a group that never saw a Christian it liked nor a criminal it didn't. Earl Warren took over as chief justice in 1953, at a time when schoolchildren across America were exposed to some religious matter in schools. Just a year before, the Supreme Court had heard a case brought by a New Jersey parent unhappy with the fact that five verses from the Old Testament were read each morning in every classroom because state law required it.[169] No "Jesus freaks" here: the Old Testament was chosen to offend neither Jew nor Gentile, or at least the New Jersey legislature thought so. In fact, the father of the schoolgirl in question had backing from the American Jewish Congress itself, as well as (surprise!) the American Civil Liberties Union.

The court accepted the case on appeal, but then spit it out again, ruling the cause was moot (no longer a viable issue) because the plaintiff's daughter had already graduated from school, and the facts did not support either the father's or the daughter's claim to have a "justiciable cause or controversy,"[170] and also noted that a person bringing a suit "must be able to show not only that the statute is invalid but that he has sustained or is immediately in danger of sustaining some direct injury as the result of its enforcement, and not merely that he suffers in some indefinite way in common with people generally."[171] In other words, you can't sue the

---

[169] Doremus v. Board of Education of the Borough of Hawthorne, 342 U.S. 429 (1952).

[170] This term is derived from the Constitution's Article III, Section 2.

[171] *Doremus,* 342 U.S. at 434, quoting Massachusetts v. Mellon, 262 U.S. 447, 488.

government because you just don't like the way they're spending your tax money or you don't like a specific government action; otherwise the courts would be overwhelmed. The court slammed the state of New Jersey for even accepting the case, saying that its judges at first turned down the case, "but, on pretrial conference, perhaps with premonitions of success, waived it and acquiesced in a determination of the federal constitutional question."[172]

The Supreme Court under Chief Justice Fred Vinson had a much better grasp of what was constitutional than Earl Warren's. In tossing this case out, the opinion noted, "Apparently the sole purpose and only function of plaintiffs is that they shall assume the role of actors so that there may be a suit which will invoke a court ruling upon the constitutionality of the statute."[173] That was, of course, the truth of the matter, something that the Warren court would go to great lengths to hide when the same cast of characters brought similarly flimsy cases in the future. The whole matter took just seven pages to explain, sort of like your boss telling you in response to your asking for a raise that the answer was not only no but hell no.

The dissent by William O. Douglas is a red flare of the problems to come when the Warren court took over and decided its agenda was more important than the Constitution and 150 years of legal precedent. Douglas begins by stating, "I think this case deserves a decision on the merits."[174] Huh? Yeah, well I think I deserve a new Ferrari, but where's the logic? What are my reasons, my precedent for demanding a shiny red sports car at no cost? There is none, which is why Douglas's dissent only runs two paragraphs. He says that, well, if every taxpayer in the district joined the suit, they still

> would not be able to show, any more than the two present taxpayers have done, that the reading of the Bible adds to the taxes they pay. But if they were right in their contentions on the merits, they would establish that their public schools were being deflected from the educational program for which the taxes were raised. That seems to me to be an adequate interest for the maintenance of this suit by all the taxpayers.[175]

---

[172] *Id.* at 433.

[173] *Id.* at 431.

[174] *Id.* at 435.

[175] *Id.*

Douglas was saying that *if* every taxpayer in the district had brought the suit instead of just two irreligious chumps, and *if* they were right in their contentions, *then* it would "seem" to be OK to *him* that the suit could be decided by the court. In other words, if we had some ham, we could have ham and eggs, if we had some eggs. Then he said that, well, the precedent of requiring that people bringing such a suit have more standing than just being taxpayers indeed kept the court from considering it, but *if* New Jersey passed its own rules governing whether such suits could be brought in its courts, *then* "I see nothing in the Constitution to prevent it."[176] Yeah, and *if* the Japanese Imperial Navy had not attacked Pearl Harbor in 1941, *then* we wouldn't have dropped the A-bomb on them four years later. But they did, and we did.

This quick rejection was exactly what the Supreme Court was supposed to do—keep preposterously stupid lawsuits from inspiring new laws just because a few justices thought they would fit their view of the world. If you need more proof, the court had a similar "establishment of religion case" less than two months later. This case[177] came out of New York and challenged a school program in which students were allowed "release time" to go from public school to religious centers for religious instruction. Note: no religion was being taught in the schools—the students were simply allowed to go elsewhere.

The opinion states that the only actual complaint by the plaintiffs that the plan amounted to an establishment of religion and therefore violated the First Amendment was that it "has resulted and inevitably results in the exercise of pressure and coercion upon parents and children to secure attendance by the children for religious instruction."[178] That is, atheists didn't like the fact that their kids might feel peer pressure to go to some church/synagogue/mosque during the "release time" instead of sitting at their desks doing something nonreligious in school. This, of course, didn't bother liberals fifty years later when conservative parents claimed that sex education in public schools might result in peer pressure to have early sex or that showing students homosexual sex practices might affect their kids' development. No, watching as your classmates went off to religious class in another building was far worse for a child's ego than being forced to fit a banana for a condom in school.

---

[176] *Id.* at 436.

[177] Zorach v. Clauson, 343 U.S. 306 (1952).

[178] *Id.* at 312.

The opinion clearly states, "We do not see how New York by this type of 'release time' program has made a law respecting an establishment of religion within the meaning of the First Amendment,"[179] even though "there cannot be the slightest doubt that the First Amendment reflects the philosophy that Church and State should be separated."[180] But the writer noted that the First Amendment does not say that there be a separation of church and state in every possible way. Otherwise, the writer goes on to say, police officers would not be allowed to protect churches, the term "so help me, God" would have to be taken out of courtroom oaths, and even Thanksgiving Day would have to be shorn of federal recognition because of its religious roots. "We are a religious people whose institutions presuppose a Supreme Being," the opinion notes later, and as long as government "shows no partiality to any one group," letting a state allow time for religious instruction off-campus "follows the best of our traditions," and holding otherwise would "show a callous indifference to religious groups."[181]

That opinion went along with the views of most Americans and most jurists in those days and matches what most Americans believe today: that as long as a government didn't push a specific religion and simply recognized there was a religious side to American life, nothing in the Constitution prevented governmental actions that acknowledged religion. What may surprise you is that this majority opinion was written by Justice William O. Douglas a few weeks after his dissent in *Doremus*, where he claimed that taxpayers should be allowed to sue over the reading of a few verses from the Old Testament each day in New Jersey schools. Perhaps there was enough difference in the cases for Douglas to switch sides, or perhaps he had decided that writing an opinion in favor of a certain recognition of religion by government would make it more believable when he claimed ten years later that he had seen the error of his ways and now thought complete and utter separation of church and state was correct. But of course, only a cynic or conspiracy theorist would think that.

So what changed in the intervening ten years before the court decided that religion could be kicked around like the school sissy? Americans were generally just as religious as earlier (the upheaval of the 1960s didn't start until almost halfway through the decade) and state governments were no

---

[179] *Id.* at 306.

[180] *Id.*

[181] *Id.* at 313–14.

more hostile to religion. What happened was that Earl Warren had taken over as chief justice in 1953 and built a majority of justices who thought that putting their liberal philosophy into effect was more important than following that yellowing piece of parchment called a constitution. It's no surprise that America reacted strongly to the suspension of school prayer; it went against everything they believed about the First Amendment and everything the Supreme Court had ruled on the issue for more than a century. The only surprise was that liberals claimed they were surprised that other people were surprised.

Engel v. Vitale was announced in late June 1962, conveniently during school vacations. The announcement came in a year that would include the Cuban Missile Crisis, arguably the nearest the United States ever came to nuclear war with the Soviet Union, and certainly a time when a lot of Americans were praying, even in schools. But it was soon to end.

Mr. Engel was one of ten parents who brought suit against New York City schools, claiming that morning prayer in schools "was contrary to the beliefs, religions or religious practices of both themselves and their children."[182] This sort of thing had been attempted before; schools were wise enough to allow children whose parents objected to remain silent during the prayer or leave the classroom. But this time, it wasn't enough. Despite what Justice Douglas had said about religion and government coexisting ten years earlier, the opinion by Hugo Black quickly gets to the point: "The State of New York has adopted a practice wholly inconsistent with the Establishment Clause."[183] "The religious nature of prayer," Black writes, "was recognized by Jefferson and has been concurred in by theological writers, the United States Supreme Court and state courts and administrative officials, including New York's Commissioner of Education."[184]

Once again, the Warren court "proved" its point by ignoring the real issue. Prayer is religious? Well, duh—as a later generation would say. But that was not the point. The point was whether allowing (not forcing) schoolchildren to say a prayer specially designed to offend no one constituted an official "establishment" of religion. Until this time, courts had said no and had made their point clearly and forcefully. Now, after 150 years of consistency and clarity, the Warren court said otherwise.

---

[182] Engel v. Vitale, 370 U.S. 421, 423 (1962).

[183] *Id.* at 424.

[184] *Id.* at 425.

A careful reader of Hugo Black's explanation of why the court had changed its mind might notice something typical of Warren court decisions that greatly changed long-accepted legal matters: there wasn't a damn thing in the Constitution or elsewhere to support it. Low on page 425 of the volume containing the decision, Black starts talking about the reasons for banning school prayer. *Ten full pages later,* he has not cited a single American legal precedent, and all he has done with the Constitution is to repeat its First Amendment ban on the establishment of religion by government, which until that date in 1962 was not considered as interfering with student prayer in public schools. In other words, Black is hoping to baffle us with bullshit. For liberals, that was enough.

What does Justice Black cite? Well, let's see here…how about the *Book of Common Prayer?* Black says that "was one of the reasons which caused many of our early colonists to leave England and seek religious freedom in America."[185] Of course, he then goes on to point out that the *Book of Common Prayer* was approved by Parliament. In England. In 1548. In case you're wondering, citing precedents from other nations that were put into effect 240 years before our own Constitution is not exactly considered binding on this country, but it's the best Black had. It's not bad enough that Black cites the *Book of Common Prayer* once, he does it *three more times* before moving on to quoting books mentioning "early theocratic governments in New England," books which were written in 1927, 1930, and 1947.[186] This, as far as legal precedent is considered, is the equivalent of citing the 1935 Sears catalog for reinforcement of one's arguments, perhaps by stating, "The 1935 Sears catalog sold overalls, and overall, I think I'm right."

Finally, Black mentions a Supreme Court case,[187] but not to back up his legal argument. Rather, he cites it to explain the history of an 1823 Virginia law establishing freedom from a state-approved religion. The truth is that the 1947 case Black cited specifically *allowed* the state of New Jersey to use tax money to pay for buses that took New Jersey school kids to parochial schools, figuring that doing so was a lot cheaper than educating the same kids at public schools. The final lines in the majority opinion of that 1947 case are telling, considering what Black was attempting just fifteen years later:

---

[185] *Id.* at 425.

[186] *Id.* at 427–29.

[187] Everson v. Board of Education of Ewing Township, 330 U.S. 1 (1947).

The First Amendment has erected a wall between Church and State. That wall must be kept high and impregnable. We could not approve the slightest breach. *New Jersey has not breached it here*[188] (italics added).

Hugo Black knew he could not cite previous Supreme Court decisions for support because previous Supreme Court decisions had *never* supported his view. But that was not about to stop him. He keeps mentioning the Puritans' distaste for the Church of England as an excuse for banning prayer in US public schools 340 years later, as if the Puritans would have said, "Oh yeah, before anything else, let's make sure we keep prayer out of our schools." He goes on to use James Madison's private writings against official state religions (meaning the state of Virginia) as a backing for his decision, as if James Madison would have approved of his ban on prayer in public schools.[189] Then he quotes an Act of Parliament during the reign of Edward VI (1547–53) for support, as if there had never been an American Revolution or a Declaration of Independence, and as if England itself still abided by that act. Finally, he grabs at the writings of Roger Williams, the man who founded Rhode Island because his religious views clashed with Puritanism, and then, after saying, "The history of man is inseparable from the history of religion," goes on to claim it is "neither sacrilegious nor antireligious to say that each separate government in this country should stay out of the business of writing or sanctioning official prayers."[190]

All right, but on the next page Black has to admit that the regents' prayer used in New York is not an establishment of religion and "seems relatively insignificant when compared to the governmental encroachments upon religion which were commonplace 200 years ago"—which, remember, was previous to our independence and Constitution, and is about all he is able to cite for precedent. He also has to say that his decision does not mean God must be taken out of the Declaration of Independence or "officially espoused anthems."[191] It's just that, well, he doesn't want New York or any other state to have school prayer. Which he can't even come out and say—rather he just closes quickly with "the judgment of the Court

---

[188] *Id.* at 18.

[189] "Memorial and Remonstrance against Religious Assessments." Black cites a book now out of print but the essay is available at: http://www.constitution.org/jm/17850620_remon.htm.

[190] *Engel,* 370 U.S. at 435.

[191] *Id.* at 435, Footnote 21.

of Appeals for New York is reversed and the cause remanded for further proceedings not inconsistent with this opinion."[192] After all that, Black doesn't even have the courage to say he is banning school prayer—just that he is reversing a New York decision that *allowed* school prayer as it had been allowed for more than a century.

With no precedent and no real statement of what it was doing, the Warren court stabbed school prayer in the back, beginning the destruction of public schooling as it was known for a hundred years. It wasn't the first time the highest court in the land was telling local school districts what they could and could not do, but it was a clear sign that no one could predict *how* the court would rule in the future, considering the lack of precedent for the *Engel* decision. In 1969, the last year of Earl Warren's time as chief justice, the court took on student speech in *Tinker v. Des Moines Independent Community School District*.[193] The court decided there that, well, school administrators could exercise *some* control over the speech of students, but they had to allow students to wear black armbands to protest the Vietnam War. That may seem like a clear distinction to the court, but look at it from the educators' viewpoint: what sort of control could they exert over students that wouldn't lead to an expensive lawsuit, financed by the always-willing ACLU? It was better just to let the students run wild, and most school districts did exactly that.

In 1986, another lawsuit allowed the court to tell school librarians what they had to put on the shelves.[194] Constitutional authority Erwin Chemerinsky, in reviewing the case, noted it was "difficult to imagine any permissible justification for a school library to remove from its shelves books by authors such as Kurt Vonnegut, Desmond Morris, Langston Hughes or Eldridge Cleaver. On the other hand, no court would require that an elementary school library purchase *Hustler* magazine."[195] But why not? If the court could decide to ban school prayer based on no precedent, there was no guarantee it wouldn't do almost anything. Why not decide little children have First Amendment rights to pornography, especially when the court didn't have the courage to call *Hustler* pornography anymore?

School districts had become wounded buffaloes, staggering around and being picked off by any public-interest lawyer who wanted to get his name

---

[192] *Id.* at 436.

[193] *Tinker*, 393 U.S..

[194] Board of Education, Island Trees Union Free School District v. Pico, 457 U.S. 853 (1982).

[195] Erwin Chemerinsky, *Constitutional Law: Principles and Policies, Second Edition* (New York: Aspen Publishers, 2002) 1112.

on the news. Each district had to defend itself at a cost of millions, but when the decisions were made, they applied to every public school in the country. For the ACLU and its pals, the US Supreme Court had become one-stop shopping, and school districts had learned that avoiding a multi-million dollar lawsuit was more important than worrying about teaching kids whose parents threatened lawsuits in every possible situation.

TAKING CHRIST OUT OF CHRISTMAS
LYNCH V. DONNELLY (1984)

The Supreme Court's war on Christmas and its decisions that make people today fearful of even *saying* "Merry Christmas" dates to the 1980s. Two cases argued or decided in 1984, *Lynch v. Donnelly* and *Wallace v. Jaffree*, defined once again what was necessary to breach the restrictions of the First Amendment's Establishment Clause,[196] and it was done, interestingly, not through the majority opinion but rather through concurrences by just one justice, Sandra Day O'Connor.

Lynch was a case technically decided in favor of religious expression, but the years since have shown that it had the opposite impact. The city of Pawtucket, Rhode Island, had a practice of putting up a Christmas display in its downtown area each year, which featured, among many other things, a crèche, or nativity scene. The many other things included "a Santa Claus house, reindeer pulling Santa's sleigh, candy-striped poles, a Christmas tree, carolers, cutout figures representing such characters as a clown, an elephant and a teddy bear, hundreds of colored lights, a large banner that

---

[196] "Congress shall make no law respecting an establishment of religion." For 150 years this was explained to mean that the United States should have no official religion, as Britain had the Church of England. The Warren and later courts decided it meant that nothing sponsored by any governmental entity could have anything to do with anything in any way religious, especially at Christmas. You decide which makes more sense.

reads 'SEASONS GREETINGS,' and the crèche [nativity scene] at issue here." It's a wonder the ACLU ever saw the crèche.

Chief Justice Burger's opinion in the five-to-four case reads as if it were written by a legally trained Billy Graham, pointing out "an unbroken history of official acknowledgement" of religion by government since at least 1789.[197] The chief justice quotes a 1973 case[198] by writing, "It has never been thought either possible or desirable to enforce a regime of total separation."[199] As examples of religion with government approval, he points out presidential proclamations of Thanksgiving, the motto "In God We Trust" on US currency, the "under God" in the Pledge of Allegiance, and even religious-themed paintings in the National Gallery. Before finding the city-owned crèche legal "when viewed in the proper context of the Christmas Holiday season," the chief justice points out that in our modern society, "an absolutist approach in applying the Establishment Clause is simplistic and has been uniformly rejected by the Court," a phrase so out-of-step with the court's direction at that time as to practically suck the eyeballs out of moderately observant readers.

Burger tried to do what he could, but it was Justice O'Connor's concurrence that made the difference in the long run. Confusing a ban on "establishment" of religion (setting up an official national religion) with "endorsement," O'Connor focuses on government endorsement of religion, stating that it "sends a message to non-adherents that they are outsiders, not full members of the political community, and an accompanying message to adherents that they are insiders, favored members of the political community."[200] But despite that, she finds the Pawtucket crèche display legal because the city "did not intend to convey any endorsement of Christianity or disapproval of non-Christian religions."[201] So, after stating that endorsement should be the criterion in Establishment Clause cases, she decides that the crèche was legal because Pawtucket didn't *mean* to endorse Christianity.[202]

So according to her, the crucial difference was between objectivity—did the government endorse religion—and subjectivity—did the government *intend* to endorse religion? That difference would take the high court

[197] Lynch v. Donnelly, 465 U.S. 668, 674 (1984).

[198] Nyquist v. Comm. for Public Educ. & Religious Liberty, 413 U.S. 756 (1973).

[199] See Lynch, 465 U.S. at 673 (quoting Nyquist, 413 U.S. at 760).

[200] Lynch, 465 U.S. at 688.

[201] Id. at 691.

[202] Id. at 692 (O'Connor, J., concurring) (stating "Pawtucket's display of its crèche, I believe, does not communicate a message that the government intends to endorse the Christian beliefs represented by the crèche.").

out of the business of examining facts and put it into the business of reading minds, an opportunity for endless mischief. O'Connor's mugwump, matronly, can't-we-all-get-along viewpoint produced a test that took the somewhat objective standards from an earlier court decision on religion, *Lemon v. Kurtzmann*—purpose of the mention of religion, effect of mentioning it, and entanglement between government and religion—and mushed them up into something that could be used to accomplish about anything with the Establishment Clause.

A year later, she did it again in *Wallace v. Jaffree*,[203] saying her endorsement test keeps government "from conveying or attempting to convey a message that religion or a particular religious belief is favored or preferred."[204] As one commentator noted, "upon examination therefore, the concept of endorsement seems both elusive and elastic."[205] In less formal language, like Grandma's girdle, the endorsement-of-religion test can be stretched to cover just about anything.

Remember that the Supreme Court had *allowed* a nativity scene in Providence in the *Lynch* case, but O'Connor's concurrence seemed to take it over. Note the way the Sixth Circuit approached a crèche case just a year later in *ACLU v. Birmingham*.[206] Rather than quoting from Chief Justice Burger's *Lynch* opinion, Chief Judge Lively quotes Justice O'Connor's endorsement theory, adding that "a majority of the Supreme Court appears to have adopted this approach."[207] Oh yeah? Then why did the *Lynch* case go against it and allow the nativity scene? By 1989, a frustrated Justice Kennedy wrote in his dissent to *Allegheny v. ACLU*[208] that the majority had objected to display of a crèche in the Allegheny County (Pennsylvania) Courthouse "because it chooses to discard the reasoning of the *Lynch* majority opinion in favor of Justice O'Connor's concurring opinion in the case." Deciding to ignore the holding in *Lynch* while applying a concurrence, Kennedy wrote, was "quite confusing."

Honestly, the situation didn't get any better after that. By 1992, the Sixth Circuit was saying that "although this [*Lemon*] test has been

---

[203] 472 U.S. 38 (1985).

[204] *Id*. at 70.

[205] Steven D. Smith, "Symbols, Perceptions, and Doctrinal Illusions: Establishment Neutrality and the 'No Endorsement' Test," *Mich. L. Rev.* 86 (1987) 266, 276.

[206] 791 F.2d 1561 (6th Cir 1986).

[207] ACLU v. Birmingham, 791 F.2d 1561, 1563 (6th Cir. 1986).

[208] 492 U.S. 573 (1989).

questioned a number of times, it still appears to govern Establishment Clause cases,"[209] but then it bowed to Justice O'Connor's endorsement test by asking whether a reasonable observer would find a Hanukkah display on city property to be an endorsement of religion.

While the court was greatly expanding its idea of what was illegal under the Establishment Clause, some of its members tried to hold the line on standing—that is, who has the right to sue. In 1985, two residents of St. Charles, Illinois, (along with the ever-present ACLU) sued that city for decorating an aerial atop a fire station each holiday season in a way that the resulting image was a cross formed by electric lights.[210] Judge Posner's appeals court opinion made it clear that the cost of the electricity used was minuscule, so taxpayer standing was irrelevant. However, Judge Posner was willing to grant standing because the plaintiffs "have been led to alter their behavior—to detour, at some inconvenience to themselves, around streets they ordinarily use" to avoid looking at the holiday cross. Did they actually go to all that trouble just to avoid seeing a cross? Did anyone see them avoiding the area around the cross? The reality didn't matter, as the judge noted, saying the test for standing "is the good-faith allegations of the complaint, rather than what the evidence shows."

So, to get standing in an Establishment Clause case, all that's really needed these days is an unsupported claim that one altered one's behavior after being offended by something that can be considered in some way religious. It makes as much sense as suing Macy's, saying you have to detour around the store each time you shop because it has a sign stating it will prosecute shoplifters and that makes you nervous. The Eleventh Circuit went down the same road with the same results in *ACLU of Georgia v. Rabun County Chamber of Commerce*.[211] While the court cites a previous case by saying a spiritual stake in the outcome or a commitment to separation of church and state are not a substitute for actual injury, it adds that the five plaintiffs really didn't like lighted crosses, especially ones that light up a state park "almost bright enough to enable one to read at night." And besides that, two of those five plaintiffs were campers, although neither had ever camped in the park in question. The opinion staggers around for

---

[209] Americans United v. City of Grand Rapids, 980 F.2d 1538, 1543 (6th Cir. 1992).

[210] ACLU v. City of St. Charles, 794 F.2d 265 (7th Cir. 1986).

[211] 678 F.2d 1379 (1982). At least the court had enough shame to give a nod to the issue of standing, saying, "Few issues involving First Amendment analysis have engendered as much debate in recent years as the question of standing to bring an Establishment Clause claim." *Id.* at 1382.

a good six pages before it finally says that these plaintiffs suffered just as much damage as the plaintiff in the school-prayer case *Abington v. Schempp* in 1963, so they would grant standing.

As another example, consider *Hewitt v. Joyner.*[212] The case deals with a piece of land in California a man willed to the county to use as a park. The land had thirty-six statues scattered around it weighing four to sixteen tons—statues that told the story of the life of Christ from the New Testament. The will stipulated that the statues were to stay on the property, which outraged the ACLU. How dare a person leave land with religious statues on it to a government agency! The case ended up in the Ninth Circuit Court of Appeals in 1990, where two of the plaintiffs said their injury was simply a curtailment of their right to use the park, and the court's opinion agreed that "standing may be based on finding that the plaintiff has been injured due to his or her not being able to move freely in public areas."[213] The same court faced a similar situation in 1996 when a group called the American Jewish Congress sued the city of Beverly Hills, California, over a menorah on city property.[214] In that case, the city didn't bother to challenge the group's standing, which derived from a simple claim that the menorah "interferes with its members' rights freely to use and enjoy Beverly Gardens Park." And this was from a Jewish group.

It gets better. In a suit over a Ten Commandments monument within a La Crosse, Wisconsin, city park, the twenty-two plaintiffs complained at length, saying that just looking at the monument disturbed them emotionally, caused physical pain, emotional distress, anger, sleeplessness, queasiness, distress, and discomfort.[215] Apparently even worse (since most of them mentioned it), the monument kept them from buying sandwiches at a nearby farmers' market.[216] If you are unable to see the silliness in all this,

---

[212] Hewitt v. Joyner, 940 F.2d 1561 (9th Cir. 1991).

[213] *Id.* at 1564.

[214] Am. Jewish Cong. v. City of Beverly Hills, 90 F.3d 379 (9th Cir. 1996).

[215] See Mercier v. City of La Crosse, 276 F.Supp.2d 961, 968 (W.D. Wis. 2003) (noting "in a period of one year, [plaintiff Henry Zumach] 'lost sleep' 50 or 60 times thinking about the monument"). Another plaintiff, Maureen Freeland, complained she had "been criticized because of her opposition to the monument and experiences sleeplessness." *Id.* at 966. Plaintiff Elizabeth Ash complained that when "she does see the monument, she feels marginalized and has experienced physical pain." *Id.* Plaintiff Constance Long stated that "being in Cameron Park makes her feel queasy and less proud to be an American because she believes the city is endorsing a particular religion." *Id.* at 967. Then there was plaintiff Curt Leitz, who "was shocked to see a religious monument in a public park and became frustrated and angry." *Id.*

[216] See Mercier v. City of La Crosse, 276 F.Supp.2d 961, 966 (W.D. Wis. 2003) (pointing out "[plaintiff Angela Belcaster] no longer has lunch in the park because of the monument"). Plaintiff Maureen Freeland stated that

allow me to put it in politically correct terms: ask yourself how a federal court would rule if a group of citizens filed suit claiming that seeing a Sikh wearing a turban made them too ill to eat nearby?

The issue of allowing standing for slight reason in Establishment Clause cases continues up to the present day. Even the much-reported lawsuits brought by Michael Newdow over the phrase "under God" in the Pledge of Allegiance, while rejected for lack of standing by the Supreme Court, which noted "the general prohibition on a litigant's raising another person's legal rights, the rule barring adjudication of generalized grievances more appropriately addressed in the representative branches, and the requirement that a plaintiff's complaint fall within the zone of interests protected by the law invoked,"[217] still had enough traction to start up the road to the high court again in 2005, because the much-reversed California-wacky Ninth Circuit allowed Newdow standing to sue on behalf of his daughter in a later case even after the child's mother proved *she* had sole legal custody, and that he "retained his own right to seek redress for alleged injuries to his parental interests."[218]

"although her colleagues eat lunch at the food co-op, she does not because she does not want to walk by the monument." *Id.* Plaintiff David N. Goode claimed that "although he still shops at the food co-op, he does not buy sandwiches to eat at the park, even though he would like to." *Id.* at 967. Plaintiff Myrna Peacock complained that "she will not buy sandwiches from the co-op to eat in the park. Being near the monument makes her uncomfortable and distresses her." *Id.* Plaintiff Eric Severson mentioned he "would like to eat lunch in the farmers' market…but he does not because of the monument." *Id.* at 968.

[217] Elk Grove Unified Sch. Dist. V. Newdow, 542 U.S. 1, 12 (2004) (quoting Allen v. Wright, 468 U.S. 737, 751 [1984]).

[218] Newdow v. U.S. Congress, 383 F.Supp.2d 1229, 1235 (E.D. Cal. 2005).

F*** YOU, AMERICA
COHEN V. CALIFORNIA (1971)

If there ever was a time the Supreme Court stuck a finger in the eye of (or more appropriately, shot the finger at) the American public, it was in 1971 in *Cohen v. California*. If you weren't around at the time, it was at the absolute height of bad feeling about the war in Vietnam and between the generations. The baby boomers, ages eight to twenty-four, were telling the "Greatest Generation," ages forty-six to sixty-four, just how stupid they were at almost every turn. Protests rocked the streets, and the media couldn't do enough to amplify them (as opposed to what it does with pro-life demonstrations, for example). Amidst all this, for some reason (drugs? blackmail? radical chic?) five members of the Supreme Court decided to go along with the worst of the hippie-radical-antiwar axis and make a crucial mistake that led America into the sludge-filled fever swamp of obscenity, pornography, and drug use that we live in today.

It started with a punk named Cohen, whose parents should have taught him better, although they were more likely sending money to the ACLU to justify his bad behavior. This kid walked into the Los Angeles County Courthouse, wearing a jacket that bore the words "Fuck the Draft." Not only was it crude, it lacked any literary merit and showed his lack of sympathy for the lower classes that liberals were supposed to embrace. Notice he wasn't proclaiming "Fuck the War," but rather the draft. He didn't particularly care who else might die in Vietnam, only that *he* didn't want to die there.

Anyway, long story short, Cohen was arrested under California Penal Code 415, which at the time prohibited "maliciously and willfully disturbing the peace of quiet of any neighborhood or person...by...offensive conduct."[219] The American Civil Liberties Union couldn't wait to jump in and suborn the Constitution once again, but simply called itself *amicus curiae* ("friend of the court") and filed a brief for reversal of Cohen's conviction. But they are too modest. Cohen's case was argued by UCLA law professor Melville Nimmer, whom UCLA itself describes on its website in this way:

> As a civil liberties lawyer, Melville Nimmer won significant victories in freedom of speech cases before both the U.S. and California Supreme Courts, including the U.S. Supreme Court case, Cohen v. California in 1971 which vindicated the right of political speech to include even words deemed highly offensive to those who hear them. He sometimes spoke of his civil rights cases, which he handled without pay for the American Civil Liberties Union, as the most satisfying part of his career.[220]

What a wonderful memorial, making it possible for every eight-year-old in America to tell his elders to go fuck themselves. Making it possible for every rap artist to fuck his mother, or tell someone else to fuck his mother, or talk about "hos" and bitches and the like. Turning movies into veritable founts of fuck-yous, with the word spoken hundreds of times in less than two hours. Congratulations, Melville. I'm sure your mother was so proud.

But on to how the Supreme Court was silly enough to make this all possible. Justice John Harlan, a Warren court favorite, notes wisely that "this case may seem at first blush to be too inconsequential to find its way into our books...,"[221] but quickly goes on to add, "The issue it presents is of no small constitutional significance."[222] It is? Try as I might, I can't seem to find the word "fuck" in the United States Constitution or its amendments.

---

[219] Cohen v. California, 403 U.S. 15, 16 (1971). The full statute also prohibits "vulgar, profane or indecent language within the presence or hearing of women or children, in a loud and boisterous manner," but Cohen did not speak the words. Nevertheless, the court called it "speech."

[220] UCLA Law website, noting the annual memorial lecture for Professor Nimmer, http://www.law.ucla.edu/home/index.asp?page=837.

[221] *Cohen*, 403 U.S. at 15.

[222] *Id.*

For more than a century, the Bill of Rights applied only to the federal government; states were allowed to set their own limits, and all chose to draw the line at various obscenities, slanders, and the like. Even after the Supreme Court arrogated power to itself by claiming the Fourteenth Amendment magically took over some (but not all!) of the earlier amendments, it spent fifty years *not* claiming that such language was somehow guaranteed to everyone in a public or semipublic forum. Justice Harlan himself had to go through some tortured logic to claim that what Cohen was doing was *not* behavior that might incite others, but rather just plain speech; after all, the court had clearly noted that "fighting words" could be ruled illegal in 1942 in a decision that has never been overturned.[223] So Harlan wanders around in hopes of showing nobody really wanted to kick the crap out of the little punk at the time:

> The conviction quite clearly rests upon the asserted offensiveness of the words Cohen used to convey his message to the public. The only "conduct" which the State sought to punish is the fact of communication. Thus, we deal here with a conviction resting solely upon "speech," not upon any separately identifiable conduct which allegedly was intended by Cohen to be perceived by others as expressive of particular views but which, on its face, does not necessarily convey any message and hence arguably could be regulated without effectively repressing Cohen's ability to express himself.[224]

See? The defendant wasn't actually trying to *anger* anyone by wearing a jacket reading "Fuck the Draft," and he wasn't trying to actually be expressive of any views to overturn the draft, because Harlan runs interference for him by stating that "at least so long as there is no showing of an intent to incite disobedience to or disruption of the draft, Cohen could not...be punished for asserting the evident position on the inutility or immorality of the draft his jacket reflected."[225] That's like saying you can walk around

---

[223] Chaplinsky v. New Hampshire, 315 U.S. 568 (1942). There, the court noted that "damn racketeer" and "damn Fascist" were "epithets likely to provoke the average person to retaliation, and thereby cause a breach of the peace." Later courts have narrowed the decision, but lacked the chutzpah to overturn it.

[224] *Cohen,* 403 U.S. at 18. For liberals reading this with a 10x loupe, Harlan noted the cases United States v. O'Brien, 391 U.S. 367 (1968), and Stromberg v. California, 283 U.S. 359 (1931). These were omitted above to make reading easier.

[225] *Id.*

all day with a jacket with the n-word on the back but claim that doesn't mean you're trying to incite anyone to action. Ha-ha.

Like so many Supreme Court decisions that are contrary to reason and precedent, Justice Harlan spends most of his time explaining how, well, there are lots of cases where such behavior would be illegal or impermissible, it's just in this *tiny* exception that it is not, and of course, the exception goes on to swallow the rule. Note how many ways Harlan concedes the *opposite* of his decision:

1. "This conviction quite clearly rests on the asserted offensiveness of the words Cohen used to convey his message to the public."[226]

2. "The First and Fourteenth Amendments have never been thought to give absolute protection to every individual to speak whenever or wherever he pleases, or to use any form of address in any circumstances that he chooses."[227]

3. "This Court has also held that the States are free to ban the simple use, without a demonstration of additional justifying circumstances, of so-called 'fighting words'...inherently likely to provoke violent reaction."[228]

So how does Harlan justify all this? By saying that Cohen didn't actually get the crap kicked out of him in the courthouse. No, really. The fact that people in the courthouse were *too civilized* to physically abuse this little twerp for wearing the jacket was used as an excuse to allow him to do so:

> While the four-letter word displayed by Cohen in relation to the draft is not uncommonly employed in a personally provocative fashion, in this instance it was clearly not "directed to the person of the hearer." No individual actually or likely to be present could reasonably have regarded the words on appellant's jacket as a direct personal insult. Nor do we have here an instance of the exercise of the State's police power to prevent a speaker from intentionally provoking a given group to hostile reaction. There is, as noted above, no showing that anyone who saw Cohen was in fact violently aroused or that appellant intended such a result.[229]

---

[226] *Id.* at 18.

[227] *Id.* at 19.

[228] *Id.* at 20.

[229] *Id.* References omitted for easier reading, but they are to Cantwell v. Connecticut, 310 U.S. 296, 309 (1940); Feiner v. New York, 340 U.S. 315 (1951); and Terminiello v. Chicago, 337 U.S. 1 (1949).

A few lines later, Harlan states, "There was no evidence that persons powerless to avoid appellant's conduct did in fact object to it,"[230] and then:

> We have been shown no evidence that substantial numbers of citizens are standing ready to strike out physically at whoever may assault their sensibilities with execrations like that uttered by Cohen. There may be some persons about with such lawless and violent proclivities, but that is an insufficient base...to force persons who wish to ventilate their dissident views into avoiding particular forms of expression.[231]

Since Harlan claims that people *not* attacking Cohen is a reason to allow his behavior, would a physical attack on Cohen at that time have averted this disaster? Of course not; Harlan would have simply thought up another excuse, and the poor schlubs who beat Cohen would have been sued by the selfsame ACLU that defended Cohen, and their lives would have been ruined. Besides, Harlan stated, "Those in the Los Angeles courthouse could effectively avoid further bombardment to their sensibilities simply by averting their eyes."[232]

That is one of the most subversive, damaging sentences in the history of Supreme Court decisions. "Don't like it? Don't watch" has been the snide riposte of every pornographer, cable TV programmer, and smartass kid since it was written in 1971. By saying that, Harlan would have made it acceptable for Cohen to drop his pants and defecate in the midst of the courthouse. After all, a passerby need only not watch and, oh yes, hold his nose. Knowing that, the "homeless"[233] spent the next few decades assaulting civilized people with smell, touch, speech, and action, until even the liberal backers of the ACLU grew fearful and allowed police to crack down despite court rulings.

Harlan claims that the California law under which Cohen was arrested, since it applied to the entire state, cannot be applied "to preserve an

---

[230] *Cohen,* 403 U.S. at 22.

[231] *Id.* at 23.

[232] *Id.* at 21.

[233] This is not a correct appellation by any standard except the liberal media's. Every person moving from one house to another is "homeless," but they are not drunken drug users who spurn civilization because they want to, or at least until it's cold enough that they'll accept the charity of a codependent liberal. Keep in mind that we are not doing these people favors by abetting their activities, any more than we are helping junkies by providing them with clean needles and a place to shoot up.

appropriately decorous atmosphere in the courthouse where Cohen was arrested" and not in other parts of the state. Harlan is claiming that if someone could wear a jacket with "Fuck the Draft" on it in a Northern California redwood forest or a Big Sur beach, the state has no right to keep him from doing it in a county courthouse. That is preposterous for at least two reasons. One is that no one knowingly allowed Cohen or anyone else to do it in a forest or on a beach; ergo, there is no discriminatory enforcement in courthouses for Harlan to reject. Further, dozens of Supreme Court rulings on free speech have done *exactly* what Harlan was complaining about—allowing certain speech at certain times in certain places, so much so that time, manner, and place restrictions on speech are specifically memorized by law students and law clerks alike. The court even calls it a standard for ruling, looking at "whether the speech restrictions in the injunction (i) were content neutral, (ii) were narrowly tailored to serve a significant government interest, and (iii) left open ample alternative channels for communication of the information."[234] Speech is restricted all the time despite the First Amendment. Military members can't say anything they want, schoolchildren can't say anything they want, people can't protest on private property except under certain circumstances, etc.

"Admittedly, it is not so obvious that the First and Fourteenth Amendments must be taken to disable the States from punishing public utterance of this unseemly expletive in order to maintain what they regard as a suitable level of discourse within the body politic."[235] No kidding, Justice Harlan, since the country had managed to pass 182 years under the Constitution without feeling words like fuck and shit were necessary to political debate. But suddenly, we just couldn't get along another week without them. And notice that Harlan, who had pointed out specifically that it was important that Cohen hadn't *spoken* the word, is now saying that "utterance" of the f-word is exactly what he is going to allow. Harlan continues, tripping over himself to justify use of such language under the "free speech" segment of Amendment I: "The constitutional right of free expression is powerful medicine in a society as diverse and populous as ours."[236] "To many, the immediate consequence of this freedom may often appear to be only verbal tumult,

---

[234] The court does this in many opinions, but this one is from Schenck v. Pro-Choice Network of Western N.Y., 519 U.S. 357, 369 (1997).

[235] *Cohen*, 403 U.S. at 23.

[236] *Id.* at 24.

discord and even offensive utterance...that the air at times may seem filled with verbal cacophony is, in this sense, not a sign of weakness but of strength."[237] Oh, bullshit, as Justice Harlan has allowed me to write. Has such language actually made our political discourse *better* in the past forty years? Hasn't his approval of such license simply made things worse all around, since such language is both insulting and too imprecise to be used in any rational debate?

And let's make something clear—whatever later justices wanted to claim, "free speech" was never meant to refer to obscenity, profanity, or the waggling of naked derrieres in front of horny males in tittie bars. Akhil Reed Amar, a constitutional expert at Yale Law School, points out that "the First Amendment took the British idea of Parliamentary 'freedom of speech and debate' and ultimately extended that freedom to all Americans."[238] What he wrote is what the framers were thinking when they drew up the original Bill of Rights—that freedom of speech meant freedom for all citizens to discuss or advocate political change, a stark difference from the old British concept that allowed members of Parliament to say whatever they wished about changing things, but not Joe Average.

This was made even clearer by a nasty dustup that followed the Bill of Rights by just a decade. The Alien and Sedition Act was passed to protect government officials from criticism by making it a criminal act for the public to criticize an incumbent officeholder (but not a candidate!). The restriction was clearly aimed at the freedom just granted the public to take government into their own hands (remember "We the People"?). Enacted in 1798, the act would punish a citizen

> if any persons shall unlawfully combine or conspire together, with intent to oppose any measure or measures of the government of the United States...or to impede the operation of any law of the United States, or to intimidate or prevent any person holding a place or office in or under the government of the United States, from undertaking, performing or executing his trust or duty,

But wait! There's more!

---

[237] *Id.* at 23–4.

[238] Akhil Reed Amar, *The Bill of Rights*, (New Haven, CT: Yale University Press, 1998), 25.

That if any person shall write, print, utter or publish, or shall cause or procure to be written, printed, uttered or published... any false, scandalous and malicious writing or writings against the government of the United States, or either house of the Congress of the United States, or the President of the United States...or to bring them, or either of them, into contempt or disrepute; or to excite against them, or either or any of them, the hatred of the good people of the United States, or to stir up sedition within the United States, or to excite any unlawful combinations therein, for opposing or resisting any law of the United States, or any act of the President of the United States...[239]

The punishment for this, by the way, could have been a fine of up to $5,000 (in real money, not the trash we pass today) and five years in jail. Luckily, the citizens voted these scoundrels out and replaced them with a somewhat less odious bunch of scoundrels in the 1800 elections, and the new group let the acts expire. But note what the laws were aimed at doing: preventing people from criticizing any new law or the Congress or president that approved or executed it. *This* is clearly what the First Amendment guarantee of free speech was meant to allow—not every f-word and compound f-word anyone can blabber on the street or television.

So what *should* control use of such language? Custom. Those who say there are only 7 words out of 250,000 or so in our language that are banned often ask why; I would ask, why not? It's not like a ban would cut down on the expression of the average person; allowing such language has actually reduced the variety of expression and increased the bad feelings, bar fights, and shootings over who disrespected whom. If necessary, any given state could pass laws over use of such language, just as California had, to preserve public dignity and even public health. If it's illegal to spit on the sidewalk for fear of spreading possibly deadly disease, why can't it be illegal to speak some words loudly and publicly that clearly inflame others and lead to violence or heart attacks?

The proof of this is in the current debate over the "n-word," as people are required to say these days. No law prevents anyone from going out on the street corner and yelling the word all day long, and yet no one does it (and survives) because it's considered insulting and demeaning; in other words, the public custom is that it is wrong to say it. Here we are in the twenty-first

---

[239] Alien and Sedition Acts, adopted July 14, 1798.

century, tiptoeing around that word in public and private, with people losing jobs over the slightest suggestion they may have said the word at one time years before, when every child in America can go around saying fuck this or that all day. *This* is what the Constitution was created for?

The dissent to *Cohen v. California* is short and to the point. Justice Blackmun authored it, backed by Hugo Black and new Chief Justice Warren Burger. Blackmun says what should have been obvious to all nine justices—that "Cohen's absurd and immature antic, in my view, was mainly conduct and little speech."[240] He also mentions the "fighting words" decision of the court in *Chaplinsky v. New Hampshire*,[241] "where Justice Frank Murphy, a known champion of First Amendment freedoms, wrote for a unanimous bench, "as a consequence, this Court's agonizing over First Amendment values seems misplaced and unnecessary."[242] "Agonizing" is a term of art used by justices to note that someone they are disagreeing with has gone to great effort to twist the Constitution into the shape they want to make their preconceived decision seem reasonable; it makes it easier than having fistfights in the Supreme Court dining room.

Blackmun then throws in a last-chance offer for the court to avoid ruining the public demeanor by noting that the California Supreme Court had, just a month after it refused to review the Cohen case, taken up another case involving the same law, in which it noted that such behavior might be acceptable if it wasn't willful conduct that is violent and endangers the public safety. Blackmun said hey, why not just send it back[243] to California and let them make the final decision? What he didn't need to say was that such a decision would avoid making *"Fuck You, America"*[244] the law of all fifty states and leave a little power to each state to decide what it wants. But of course, that's not what the whacked-out liberal activists on the Supreme Court and the ACLU desired—they *wanted* to have a fuck-you America, and so we got it.

Which leaves the question of *why* such an outcome was desired so strongly by the ACLU. Their genius-level attorneys no doubt knew that

---

[240] *Cohen*, at 27.

[241] 315 U.S. 568 (1942).

[242] *Id.*

[243] The legal term is *remand*; hence the use of the phrase "reverse and remand" in many court rulings. That is, they are saying you lower court guys made a mistake earlier, here's the same case back and please try to decide it differently.

[244] Oops, pardon me—I meant Cohen v. California.

adding this sort of contentious language to the common vocabulary of every child and submoron was going to neither help political discourse nor improve public behavior—could it be they simply hoped to damage the nation? Perhaps, because there's very little evidence that the outcome of *Cohen v. California* did anything else.

THROWING OUT THE BABY, WITH OR WITHOUT BATHWATER
ROE V. WADE (1973)

As every law student is required to learn, there are some cases the US Supreme Court will not look into no matter what. The court will never look into a "political question"—meaning deciding on an election and the like. Well, except *Bush v. Gore* in 2000, but whattaya gonna do, huh? The court also will not consider a case unless it exhibits two key factors: standing and ripeness; and it does *not* suffer mootness.[245] Standing means the person bringing the suit has actually suffered some sort of injury; proenvironment groups have been "poured out" of court before a trial began because the members of the group hadn't actually suffered any damage from the defendant and therefore no standing existed. Ripeness is that a case has come to a point where the injury has actually occurred, and the trial could do some good; courts aren't going to hear a case involving you and the neighbor's dog just because you *think* he may bite you someday—your butt actually has to bleed before you've got a case. And mootness is basically the opposite—it's too late for a court to come in and decide the case because the cat is out of the bag and can't be stuffed back in, assuming you have no

---

[245] These are also referred to as injury, causation, and redressability, meaning the specific person who brings the suit has been injured, the person (which can also be a corporation under our laws) being sued has done something to cause it, and issuing an injunction or fining the defendant will actually help return the plaintiff to the point he was before the injury (redressability). *Source:* Erwin Chemerinsky, *Constitutional Law* (New York: Aspen Publishers, 2001).

continuing injury. Say, hypothetically, you want to put a new political party on the ballot, but the state government thinks of some reason not to accept your petitions until the election is over.[246] At that time, the issue is moot, since it's too late to affect the election. Such it is with pregnancy—why take a case involving abortion when the woman has already had the child?

Why, indeed. The court had its excuse ready, one used a few times before. If a problem is "capable of repetition, yet evading review,"[247] the court can still take it up. What few people notice is how quickly and eagerly the Supreme Court "took up" the case of *Roe v. Wade*. You likely know that cases have to work their way up the ladder to the Supreme Court—you can't have a case before a lowly federal district court and then jump all the way to the Supreme Court; one would at least have to stop at the Court of Appeals for your area.

Well, except for *Roe v. Wade*. The liberal members of the court were so anxious to grab this case and change the law nationwide that they didn't even let the Fifth Circuit Court of Appeals get its hands on it. Instead, the Fifth Circuit "ordered the appeals held in abeyance pending decision here."[248] As if the Fifth Circuit could tell the US Supreme Court to take a case while it twiddled its thumbs. Nope, it's clear who was handing out marching orders here. Even worse, as far as the legal system is concerned, the defendant in the case[249] had not even asked the Supreme Court to take it up after he lost in the lower court. Justice Harry Blackmun noted that "it might have been preferable" if Henry Wade's team had asked the Supreme Court to look at it; but no problem, Blackmun decided, it was going to get here sooner or later anyway, so let's get on with it.[250]

And that wasn't the only eye-popping part of the case. As the Warren court had done until 1969, the new court was willing to make up laws from thin air, or at least write opinions that used mostly their own recent decisions to justify themselves, with occasional forays into laws that existed before the

---

[246] OK, it's not hypothetical; this is a real case. Moore v. Ogilvie, 394 U.S. 814 (1969).

[247] Southern Pacific Terminal Co. v. ICC, 219 U.S. 498, 515 (1911).

[248] Roe v. Wade, 410 U.S. 113, 123 (1973).

[249] Henry Wade, district attorney of Dallas County, Texas, in 1973. Since Wade was in charge of criminal prosecutions in the county, he was the guy who got sued in such a case. Wade is also remembered for being the DA who would have prosecuted Lee Harvey Oswald for the Kennedy assassination in 1963, and who did prosecute Jack Ruby for shooting Oswald two days later.

[250] Want my theory? Richard Nixon had been reelected just two months before the Roe v. Wade decision, and Nixon was determined to put conservatives on the court. Ergo, Blackmun and his liberal buddies figured *Roe* was a rush job, lest one of the leftists on the court keel over and get replaced by someone less free with the interpretation of the Constitution.

Constitution and had been replaced when the Constitution was adopted. Blackmun outlines "the principal thrust of [Roe]'s attack" and it includes the usual suspects: *Griswold v. Connecticut*,[251] discussed earlier, in which the court set the table for *Roe*, and *Eisenstadt v. Baird*,[252] decided by the same court just a few months before. Then Blackmun uses the other trick: "Before addressing this claim, we feel it desirable briefly to survey...the history of abortion, for such insight that history may afford us." Translation: we know the Constitution doesn't say jack squat about abortion, and no court said anything on point until we decided to do it, so I'm just hoping to baffle you with stuff that happened before the United States existed.

Which he attempts, going from the Persian Empire, through the Hippocratic oath (which forbade abortion), an explanation that abortion before the sixteenth week or so was not a crime in England in 1762, and that US states followed that common law until the mid-nineteenth century. That's a nice historical perspective, but it has nothing to do with our Constitution or the state of medicine in 1973. Certainly early abortion was not a crime until the mid-nineteenth century—most women never saw a doctor, the embryo was so small it might not be found for evidentiary reasons, such things were not discussed in public, birth statistics were rarely kept, and it was difficult at the time to tell a miscarriage from an abortion. It's sort of like saying Internet fraud wasn't a crime until the 1990s, so why make it one now?

Blackmun finally gets around to the American Medical Association, which had opposed legalized abortion until 1970, when it finally gave a tentative OK. To which I must say, "So what?" The AMA isn't a legislative body that actually can enact or repeal laws, so you might as well be quoting the California Fruit Board for support. And besides, the AMA's guidelines had called for "sound clinical judgment" and "best interests of the patient," specifically noting that an abortion should not be performed through "mere acquiescence to the patient's demand,"[253] which is exactly what the court was about to allow. So even the American Medical Association wasn't *actually* behind Blackmun's plan.

Blackmun then notes that it "has been argued occasionally that those laws were the product of a Victorian social concern to discourage illicit

---

[251] 381 U.S. 479 (1965).

[252] 405 U.S. 438 (1972).

[253] *Roe*, 410 U.S. at 143.

sexual conduct."[254] *Who* argued that? Blackmun doesn't say because he's only throwing that in as a straw man, setting up an argument that no one has made in order to make himself look better. Then he says the pro-abortion side claims "that this is not a proper state purpose at all."[255] That is, discouraging illicit sexual conduct. Which no one claimed was a reason, anyway.

Of course, what Blackmun doesn't mention as a "proper state purpose" is continuing the nation's existence by assuring that there will be a next generation, and more to the point, assuring that soon-to-be citizens not be murdered by the thousands. In a nation where eco-freaks chain themselves to trees to keep them from being cut down and people demand that dog pounds never kill another pooch, it's strange that so many people think abortion should be legal right up to the date of birth.[256]

Blackmun's opinion then notes that legislative histories of many anti-abortion laws show more concern with the mother's health than the child's, but again, these laws were passed in a time when people *couldn't* be too concerned about a child's health, since so many of them died before age five. And besides, what does a legislative history have to do with anything? That's simply a record of what *didn't* get passed into law as the legislators argued over various parts of what would become the law; it's better to simply read the law they passed, which actually carries legal weight, and decide what they meant by it.

Finally, Blackmun gets to the meat of his argument, saying, "The Constitution does not explicitly mention any right of privacy."[257] Well, like, duh. But Blackmun cites a raft of Warren-era decisions in which the court had already broken sharply with precedent and the Constitution, and throws in a few other cases to confuse matters (*Boyd v. United States*,[258] mentioned earlier, which dealt with ownership of a plate-glass shipment for tax purposes, and *Olmstead v. United States*,[259] which Blackmun can only quote for support from Justice Brandeis's dissent,[260] not the actual decision that became law).

---

[254] *Id.* at 148.

[255] *Id.*

[256] Gallup has polled this issue since *Roe.* In 1993, 34% of respondents believed abortions "should be legal under any circumstances." The number dropped to 25% by 2011, but that's still tens of millions of people.

[257] *Roe,* 410 U.S. at 152. Note that he's almost forty pages into this opinion, and he's just getting to the kernel.

[258] 116 U.S. 616 (1886).

[259] 277 U.S. 438 (1928).

[260] I've noted it before, but I'll say it again: dissents are not part of the "law" of the case, which comes only from the majority opinion. Quoting a dissent may give one comfort but not support, legally.

Then Justice Byron "Whizzer" White chimes in with a concurrence. Interestingly, while he and Blackmun are quick to decide the Constitution gives us a right to privacy without actually saying so, White is very slow to find that the Constitution allows unborn children to be persons. In fact, he says the Constitution "does not define person in so many words." Yeah, and it didn't say black people were persons either, as the Dred Scott decision showed, but was changed in the years following. At least White admits why he can't find personhood in the Constitution—"if this suggestion of personhood is established, [Roe's] case, of course, collapses." Can't have that happening, can we?

White then says that the Texas law allowing abortion only to save the life of the mother "sweeps too broadly" because it "makes no distinction between abortions performed early in pregnancy and those performed later, and it limits to a single reason, 'saving' the mother's life." So you see, the law "sweeps too broadly" because *it is too restrictive!* And speaking of sweeping broadly, isn't the decision to make abortion available anytime anywhere in all fifty states without Constitutional justification sort of "sweeping broadly"? I mean, just a little bit?

Finally, the majority decides that abortion must be faced in three segments. For the first trimester, mom and the doctor can flush the little bastard out, no questions asked. In the second trimester (months four through six), the state is allowed to "regulate the abortion procedure in ways that are reasonably related to maternal health." And finally, in the last three months, states are allowed to ban abortion except to save the life of the mother.

Bet you didn't know all that was in the decision. That's because it was thrown in as a sop to the states and Catholics, and nobody ever paid attention to it again. The court had become the doctors *and* the lawyers, making medical decisions with a broad sweep no real doctor would attempt. Not only did Blackmun set medical standards for abortions, he also barred physicians from doing so. "Allowing a panel of doctors to consider whether an abortion was needed," Blackmun said, "is an unconstitutional complication."[261] We must admit that if the Constitution didn't mention abortion, it likely also did not mention physicians' opinions thereof. This reasoning could lead to some interesting outcomes. If physicians aren't needed to help make the decision to get a medically complicated and possibly dangerous procedure

---

[261] "A Stunning Approval for Abortion," *Time*, February 5, 1973.

such as an abortion, why not extend it to heart transplants, brain surgery, sex changes, and so on? If a woman is in charge of her body, why stop at abortions? And yet, for some reason, they did. After all, these women who demand abortions when they want them ignore the fact that they have no legal right to demand that their gall bladder come out on demand.

For once, the reaction to the decision was instant and strong. Those for abortion (I mean "pro-choice") celebrated, while those opposed to abortion (I mean "pro-life") proclaimed the end of civilization. It's wise to note what some highly respected doctors had to say at the time, though. Take Dr. Landrum B. Shettles, who wrote to *The New York Times* a week after the decision:

> A new composite individual is started at the moment of fertilization. However, to survive, an individual needs a very specialized environment for the first nine months, just as it requires sustained care for an indefinite period after birth. But from the moment of the union of the germ cells [egg and sperm], there is under normal development a living, definite, going concern. To interrupt a pregnancy at any stage is like cutting the link of a chain; the chain is broken no matter where the link is cut. Naturally, the earlier the pregnancy is interrupted, the easier it is technically, the less the physical, objective encounter. To deny a truth should not be made a basis for legalizing abortion.[262]

Dr. Shettles was not your ordinary country doctor or fundamentalist chump. Born in 1909, he received his masters of science degree in 1934, his PhD from Johns Hopkins in 1938, and his MD in 1943. In 1951, he became the first person to achieve *in vitro* fertilization (taking it to birth was still twenty-seven years away), invented chorionic villi sampling for genetic testing in 1969, and developed the Gamete Intrafallopian Transfer method (GIFT) in 1978.[263] He was telling the public that just because an early abortion made it simpler and easier, it didn't change the fact that it killed a human.

But keep in mind that legal abortion already existed in the United States in those states that actually wanted it. What the Supreme Court did

---

[262] "Letters to the Editor," *New York Times*, February 14, 1973.

[263] Website of Landrum B. Shettles, http://landrumshettles.com/biography.html.

was force completely unrestricted abortion on the forty-six states that *didn't* want it. Remember, all of these states' legislatures had specifically passed laws involving abortion; some were quite restrictive (as in Texas, where *Roe v. Wade* arose), and four (New York, Washington, Hawaii, and Alaska) allowed unrestricted abortions.[264] So much for our republican form of government—that is, the idea of electing representatives to deal with the difficult questions and getting different answers in different states. Better just to let the Supreme Court make all the decisions for us.

The media, of course, loved it. Although the year was too crowded with big news to allow *Roe v. Wade* to be a cover story (Vietnam, Watergate, energy crisis, inflation), *Time* slotted two stories into its law section. One, "The Decision Blow by Blow," explained how the issue was argued in late 1971, but new Justice Harry Blackmun took so long to write the opinion that it dragged into the next Supreme Court term and had to be reargued in October 1972. "Nevertheless, for 13 months while the issue raged...and countless women suffered personal tragedy, the court remained silent."[265] Maybe my thirty-plus years in journalism make media bias show up more clearly to me, but did you notice the automatic assumption that it was the Supreme Court's job to overturn the laws of all fifty states when it felt like it, and that the decision better be the one liberals wanted? And worse, note that statement that "countless women suffered personal tragedy" while they waited. And what would that "personal tragedy" have been? *Having a child.* It certainly couldn't have been dying of an illegal abortion, as so many feminists have warned over the years. Not only was that not "countless women," the number was easily counted. The Centers for Disease Control reported that sixty-five women died from abortions in 1972, but not in back alleys—in fact, twenty-four of those who died had received *legal* abortions, versus thirty-nine who died in illegal abortions[266] (two were unknown as to legality).

While backers of abortion tended to center on the poor unmarried woman forced into a back alley through no fault of her own, only to die with a coat hanger in her uterus, the reality that followed *Roe v. Wade* was quite different and even more troubling. Few people are aware that Margaret Sanger founded Planned Parenthood in large part to convince minorities

---

[264] "A Stunning Approval for Abortion," *Time*, February 5, 1973.

[265] "The Decision Blow by Blow," *Time*, February 5, 1973.

[266] Laurie D. Elam-Evans, PhD, et al., "Abortion Surveillance—United States, 2000," Centers for Disease Control and Prevention, *Morbidity and Mortality Weekly Report* 52, no. SS-12 (2003).

and lower-class women to have fewer children. The Supreme Court must have been reading her mind. While whites received 55 percent of the abortions in 2002, blacks got 36 percent of them, and considering that blacks were just 12 percent of the population that year, it's clear that they were getting abortions at three times the rate of whites. Even worse, the percentage of pregnancies ending in abortion was much higher for blacks than whites. "The abortion ratio for black women (495 per 1,000 live births) was 3.0 times the ratio for white women (164 per 1,000)."[267] Forget Margaret Sanger—the Ku Klux Klan itself couldn't have hoped for more.

As for the image of heartbroken single women abandoned by evil men, there is plenty of evidence that single women got more abortions—about 80 percent of abortions were performed on unmarried women. But nonetheless it's troubling how many married women chose to have abortions, indicating that they were simply using abortion as a form of birth control— about 200,000 of them a year.[268] More evidence for the use of abortion as birth control is that the percentage of abortions for women younger than nineteen went from 33 percent in 1973 to 20 percent in 2000, while that for women over twenty-five went from 35 percent to 48 percent. It's obvious that the reason for the pregnancy wasn't ignorance but convenience, since teenagers seemed to be learning to avoid pregnancy better than older women during those twenty-seven years.

Perhaps most troubling is the CDC's statement that "for 1972–2000, a total of 470 abortion-related deaths were reported in the 2001 abortion *MMWR Surveillance Summary*."[269] But of course, that is not the truth. Oh, to be sure, 470 pregnant women died from legal abortions. But pro-lifers would point out almost *50 million* unborn children[270] died from abortion-related deaths in that time, too. Even pro-choice advocates would have to admit that the *potential* for 50 million Americans died, meaning we may have lost about 17 percent of our nation's economy to abortion. That would be worth about an extra $400 billion to the federal government's tax revenues, and $2 *trillion* to our Gross Domestic Product. That could also be the reason some 12 million–20 million aliens have poured into the United

---

[267] *Id.*

[268] *Id.*

[269] Lilo T. Strauss, MA, et al., "Abortion Surveillance—United States, 2002," Centers for Disease Control and Prevention, *Morbidity and Mortality Weekly Report* 54, no. SS-7 (2005).

[270] Results calculated from Strauss, et al., "Abortion Surveillance—United States, 2002." Actual abortion figures added through 2002, then 850,000 a year (somewhat less than the average in recent years) added for 2003–07.

States to take jobs "nobody else wants." Could be that the "nobodies" who didn't want the jobs simply didn't survive to get them.

Is this an anti-abortion screed? No, I would simply like to see the individual states have control over their own destinies. But I am pointing all this out to show what a magnificent arrogance that earlier Supreme Court had when it forced states to accept abortion under any circumstances. Not concerning itself with the future, the court claimed to see an illusory "privacy" right that it thought only affected the women involved; they missed considering the huge cost (literally) it would later have on the rest of us.

SHAKING MY NAKED ASS IS FREE SPEECH—GOT A PROBLEM WITH THAT?CITY OF ERIE V. PAP'S A.M. (2000)

It took just nine years for the Supreme Court to go from allowing governments to ban nude dancing to telling them that naked table dances were protected speech. The result has been to clothe businesses that sell nudity (and often sex and drugs) in the garb of the First Amendment. It might be worth it to check on what the framers of the Constitution would say about that, since such dancing wasn't known to be a public entertainment in the 1780s,[271] but that's certainly not the way of modern Supreme Court justices, who give more sway to what they burp from breakfast than what the founders of this nation might have meant when it comes to the Constitution.

Like most other major cases decided by the Supreme Court in recent years, nude dancing was one of those things state and local governments were allowed to decide on before the court took it up. Places like New Orleans and Las Vegas were permissive; places like Dubuque and Sioux Falls were not. As late as 1991, in *Barnes v. Glen Theatre, Inc.,*[272] the court favored the rights of states to decide. The opinion seems a little silly, as it begins by stating "The Kitty Kat Lounge, Inc. (Kitty Kat) is located in the city

---

[271] However, one gets the feeling that Ben Franklin would have supported it.

[272] 501 U.S. 560 (1991).

of South Bend. It sells alcoholic beverages and presents 'go-go dancing.' Its proprietor desires to present 'totally nude dancing,' but an applicable Indiana statute regulating public nudity requires that the dancers wear 'pasties' and a 'G-string' when they dance."

But behind the silliness is an argument that hangs over most Supreme Court cases in the last half of the twentieth century: who gets to make these decisions, the elected officials of states and cities, or unelected federal judges who can't be fired? Of course, the backers of ass-shaking in the name of free speech[273] wanted it presented another way, which is that ass-shaking in a G-string is merely free speech of a sort, and forcing the strippers to wear G-strings is muzzling free speech.[274]

The general subject of obscenity once almost made sense. In 1957 the court heard *Roth v. United States*,[275] which actually was a New York and a California case mashed together. Both defendants were guilty of advertising sexually oriented publications through the mails. Was this free speech that should be allowed? Justice Brennan made it clear in his opinion that it certainly was not and never had been:

> It is apparent that the unconditional phrasing of the First Amendment was not intended to protect every utterance. This phrasing did not prevent this Court from concluding that libelous utterances are not within the area of constitutionally protected speech.At the time of the adoption of the First Amendment, obscenity law was not as fully developed as libel law, but there is sufficiently contemporaneous evidence to show that obscenity, too, was outside the protection intended for speech and press. The protection given speech and press was fashioned to assure unfettered interchange of ideas for the bringing about of political and social changes desired by the people.[276]

The two defendants were fined and the world kept turning for a few years without being buried in obscenity. Then the sixties hit, and the court was as affected by the decade as the rest of the country. In 1968 the court heard

---

[273] Among the usual suspects involved in the case were the ACLU and People for the American Way. Ergo, these days the "American way" must include staring at twitching naked buttocks.

[274] What a G-string actually muzzles, I'd rather not discuss.

[275] 354 U.S. 476 (1957).

[276] Beauharnais v. Illinois, 343 U.S. 250, 266 (1952).

Interstate Circuit v. Dallas. The city of Dallas had a movie-reviewing board that decided whether children sixteen and under could see certain movies, with anything likely to "incite delinquency or sexual promiscuity"[277] getting the thumbs down. Wait a minute, the court said, that rule is too vague because you haven't specified what delinquency or sexual promiscuity are, so they smacked down the review board. That was just a windup to the case of *Miller v. California* in 1973.[278] Like some other disastrous court decisions, this one appeared to give conservatives what they wanted; it just made it so hard to achieve their goals that few would bother. The opinion states that "obscene material is not protected by the First Amendment." Even better, Chief Justice Burger's opinion specifically notes, "It is neither realistic nor constitutionally sound to read the First Amendment as requiring the people of Maine or Mississippi to accept public depiction of conduct found tolerable in Las Vegas or New York City."[279] That seems to fit with allowing states to set their own standards for obscenity. Ah, but what *is* obscene? There's the rub! Burger lays down a three-part test for obscenity:

1. Whether the average person applying contemporary community standards, would find that the work, taken as a whole, appeals to prurient interest.

2. Whether the work depicts or describes, in a patently offensive way, sexual conduct specifically defined by applicable state law.

3. Whether the work, taken as a whole, lacks serious literary, artistic, political, or scientific value.[280]

Now think of yourself as a district attorney in say, Maine or Mississippi. If your state passes an obscenity law to keep pornography out of your state and you want to prosecute somebody for that crime, all they have to do is pass *one* of these three tests to beat the rap. In addition, you can't nail them for any specific obscene act or portrayal if the book or movie, "taken as a whole," can pass the smell test. So, if a group of hookers wanted to do *Hamlet* completely in the nude, well, they could, because Shakespeare has "serious literary" value. And who is that "average person" who's going to decide that something appeals to "prurient interests"? No matter whom you come up with, the ACLU is going to say they're not "average," but that someone who approves of the obscenity is.

---

[277] Interstate Circuit v. Dallas, 390 U.S. 676 (1968).

[278] Miller v. California, 413 U.S. 15 (1973).

[279] *Id.* at 32.

[280] *Id.* at 24.

All in all, the Supreme Court might as well have said that prosecutors had to try these cases while wearing red noses and riding unicycles, as likely as it was going to be that the cases would be prosecuted, and even tougher, would be won and not appealed to a more "tolerant" forum. Thus for the next twenty years, "obscenity" almost disappeared.

And the case of *Barnes v. Glen Theatre* in 1991 helped finish it off. In that case, Chief Justice Rehnquist begins his opinion by discussing what really might qualify as free speech, noting a Supreme Court ruling that burning a draft card was not protected "speech."[281] The case gave rise to a test of whether the government can regulate speech under certain conditions, two of which are "if it furthers an important or substantial governmental interest; if the governmental interest is unrelated to the suppression of free expression."[282] Rehnquist writes, "Indiana's public indecency statute is justified despite its incidental limitations on some expressive activity."[283] His opinion went into the long history of bans on public nudity, going back to the common law of England. This sort of thing is quickly accepted by liberals when it's used to ban school prayer, but simply saying this and stating that Indiana's "purpose of protecting societal order"[284] is enough to allow a ban on nude dancing was not enough for them. Justice White's dissent takes Rehnquist's belief that occasionally dancing may be an expressive behavior and tries to stretch it into a rule that *any dancing* must be protected as an expressive behavior, using the weak argument that these poor strippers are being discriminated against, since "no arrests have ever been made for nudity as part of a play or ballet."[285] Yeah, and it's unlikely that the ballerinas have ever been arrested for prostitution, unlike the strippers. It's silly to try to equate ballet dancing with stripping because they are clearly done for different reasons. Perhaps some men may be aroused by a ballet, but it's not the primary point of the dance. Any judge who tries to say that lap dancing is mainly an artistic endeavor is denying several thousand years of human behavior.

Justice Scalia concurs with the Rehnquist opinion, but says it would make a lot more sense simply to say that the First Amendment is not even involved in such laws: "The First Amendment explicitly protects 'the freedom of speech [and] of the press'—oral and written speech—not 'expressive

---

[281] United States v. O'Brien, 391 U.S. 367 (1968).

[282] Barnes v. Glen Theatre, Inc., 501 U.S. 560, 567 (1991), quoting United States v. O'Brien at 376–77.

[283] *Id.*

[284] *Id.* at 568.

[285] *Id.* at 590.

conduct.'"[286] For instance, Scalia says, laws against loudness and disturbing the peace don't depend on *what* a person is saying or doing, just that it interferes with the wishes of others to be left alone. Likewise, it's silly to claim that the *content* of the nude dance involves the First Amendment. But of course, the Supreme Court as a whole has not been able to make such common-sense statements in recent years, so the nude-dancing matter was left with enough life to make it to year 2000, when Justice O'Connor wrote a particularly bad opinion that allowed it that much more life. O'Connor had become the "swing" vote on the court by then, which meant that her legal philosophy was shaky enough that it was easy for liberals to talk her into taking stands that allowed them plenty of room to make mischief, even when she *seemed* to be agreeing with conservatives. This is one of those cases, and the fact that she wrote the opinion is probably evidence that she told Chief Justice Rehnquist that he could either allow her to write it or simply lose her to the other side.

City of Erie v. Pap is another of those cases in which the court allows itself the luxury of ignoring its own rules. In general, the court is not supposed to review cases that are moot—that is, no longer have an active legal question in them or, as you'll see, an ongoing legal injury. Just because the situation at one time might have needed a high court decision is not supposed to mean the court will take a look at it, *just in case* it happens again. Otherwise the court would go through life cherry-picking cases that any four of its members thought might be useful to changing the Constitution the way they liked. In this case, the corporation named Pap's A.M. had closed down its Kandyland strip joint long before the case reached court and asked that it *not* be reviewed due to mootness. So O'Connor writes, "The city has an ongoing injury because it is barred from enforcing the public nudity provisions of its ordinance. If the challenged ordinance is found constitutional, then Erie can enforce it, and the availability of such relief is sufficient to prevent the case from being moot." I suppose you could say any governmental entity has an "ongoing injury" if it can't enforce *any* law. Texas would have an "ongoing injury" if capital punishment were ruled unconstitutional by an appeals court because it couldn't kill all two hundred-plus people currently on death row, and the federal government would have an "ongoing injury" if the IRS couldn't vacuum 100 percent of our salaries out of the bank, but things like that aren't usually enough to push a case into

---

[286] *Id.* at 576.

the Supreme Court. It's clear the court *wanted* to rule on the case. What's interesting is the way O'Connor manages to snatch defeat from the jaws of victory. After all, the strip joints technically *lost* this case, but there are more tittie bars in America today than in 2000, and all of the ones I drive past do a really good business, judging from the parking lots. The reason is the way O'Connor writes her opinion and what she chooses to base it on.

As I've said several times so far, the Supreme Court went wrong when it decided to start handing out decisions that changed the law in every state. It completely undermined the federal system that this country was built on, which allowed the states great latitude in how business and life were regulated within their borders. Instead, the court forced a single rule on every state, despite the different shapes, sizes, locations, and populations of the states.

O'Connor's mistake is based on her weak philosophical background. People with little idea of *why* they believe *what* they believe often end up trying to make everybody happy, since all the fighting and scream-ing seem so unnecessary to them. With no real philosophy, these people end up calling themselves pragmatists, as if making up stuff as you go along is some sort of actual ethos, which it isn't. And so it was with Sandra O'Connor. Rather than agree with that nasty old conservative Justice Scalia that a state regulating whether proto-hookers can shake their asses naked is its own business and certainly has nothing to do with freedom of speech, she instead tried to please everyone by saying that Justice Stevens contended that "the ordinance is related to the suppression of expression because language in the ordinance's preamble suggests that its actual purpose is to prohibit erotic dancing of the type performed at Kandyland."[287] She disagrees, but says "the ordinance does not attempt to regulate the primary effects of the expression, i.e., the effect on the audience of watching nude erotic dancing, but rather the secondary effects, such as the impacts on public health, safety, and welfare, which we have previously recognized are 'caused by the pres-ence of even one such' establishment."[288] With that, she's lost the whole caboodle, because she *has admitted the liberals were right* in calling it a First Amendment matter.

Oh yeah, she can say she disagrees with them on the impact of the First Amendment on the matter, but the horse is not only out of the barn,

---

[287] City of Erie v. Pap's A.M., 529 U.S. 277, 290 (2000).

[288] *Id.* at 291 (quoting Renton v. Playtime Theatres, Inc., 475 U. S. 41, 47–8, 50 (1986).

it's in the next county by now. Once you've set that predicate for the lawsuits, it's just a question of whether a particular lawyer can convince a particular judge or jury that his strip-club owner was safely within the First Amendment when his girls danced. It's possible that half or more of the cases will fail, but that doesn't matter. Once a plaintiff has a good chance of winning a case, cities will throw in the towel. They don't want to be the one who spends millions of taxpayers' money on a losing cause, especially when the other side is often getting free legal service from the ACLU because theirs is a "free speech" matter that can be sold to their members as another travesty of overreaching government.

So bingo! In allowing the opinion to become a First Amendment matter, O'Connor has lost the war even though she thinks she has won this battle. Saying that in "trying to control the secondary effects of nude dancing, the ordinance seeks to deter crime and the other deleterious effects caused by the presence of such an establishment in the neighborhood,"[289] O'Connor cedes that the primary effect of twitching your naked ass is free expression wrapped up with the First Amendment, something the Supreme court never bothered to worry about before the days when there was a hooker on every corner. Liberal darling Justice Souter was quick to jump in and demand that cities trying to ban nude dancing should have to pile up reams of evidence showing that such joints definitely had deleterious effects on the community even *before* the city could pass the ban.

For once, Justices Scalia and Thomas are not on the dissent side of this case, since they agreed with the basic decision that nude dancing could be banned by cities. But their concurrence has much the same sting as a dissent, pointing out in clear English that worrying about the First Amendment value of butt-shaking is preposterous: "I still would not find that this regulation violated the First Amendment unless I could be persuaded (as on this record I cannot) that it was the communicative character of nude dancing that prompted the ban."[290] Of course, it wasn't the supposed *message* of the butt-wavers that bothered Erie officials; instead it was the shaking of the butts themselves. But no one seems to have the courage these days to point out simply that dancing in the nude to arouse drunken males is not a good thing for society.

---

[289] *Id.* at 293.
[290] *Id.* at 310.

This reminds me of the movie *It's a Wonderful Life*, where George Bailey (played by Jimmy Stewart) sees what would have happened to his small town if he had not existed. Instead of the upright and hardworking outlook it had as Bedford Falls, it turns into Potterville, named after George's nemesis, played by Lionel Barrymore. Every other business is a bar or strip joint, the average worker wastes his money on wild women and liquor instead of supporting his family, and hookers walk the streets without shame. In the movie, the scene is a short nightmare for George, but our Supreme Court has made it possible for us to deal with this nightmare every day of our lives. Aren't they nice?

THE END OF NONDISCRIMINATION REGENTS OF THE UNIV. OF CALIFORNIA V. BAKKE (1978)

If there ever was a Supreme Court decision that made it clear the court had become opposed to practically everything that America stood for, it was *Bakke*. Not so much for the namesake of the case—despite what you may remember, Allan Bakke was admitted to the medical school of the University of California at Davis by order of the Supreme Court itself. It was the many ways the court had to tie the law into knots to justify the odious practice of so-called affirmative action,[291] which almost equaled what an earlier Supreme Court had done to make slavery seem justified.[292]

"Affirmative action," as used today, had thousands of defenders but almost no definers. What does it mean? In the oral arguments before the court,[293] Attorney General Archibald Cox prissily informs the court that

---

[291] Long before it was dragooned into service to be a seemingly benign name for racial discrimination, affirmative action actually meant something—action required by an employer, innkeeper, or common carrier to come to the aid of someone in peril (since normally no such action is required). Just as "ghetto" was turned from an area where some people were *forced* to live into another, less-judgmental name for "slum," the politically correct version of affirmative action has so replaced the original definition that the first is hard to find. *Black's Law Dictionary* ignores the original meaning, but see *Prosser, Wade and Schwartz's Torts, Tenth Edition*, 416–17.

[292] Dred Scott v. Sandford, 19 Howard 393 (1857). Slaves were defined as "property" to remove their human rights even after they had escaped to a nonslave state.

[293] Available on the web at http://www.oyez.org/cases/1970-1979/1977/1977_76_811/. The case was argued on Columbus Day, 1977, and two hours of oral arguments were recorded. You can listen to them.

if affirmative action is not approved, minorities would be "reduced to the trivial numbers which they were" prior to affirmative action—which would suggest that somehow most of these minority applicants were not qualified by objective standards to be admitted to medical school. But no, Cox says, he only wants the UC–Davis medical school to make a "selection among qualified applicants." But he soon admits that until 1969, grades and admissions tests "excluded almost all members of minority groups." Note that he didn't say *discrimination* excluded them, but rather objective measures of grades and test scores. While fewer than 1 percent of medical students nationwide were black[294] in the academic year 1968–69, the UC–Davis administration had used affirmative action to raise overall minority enrollment to sixteen of one hundred admitted students in the mid-1970s. In his argument Cox was quick to say these people were still "fully qualified." Now, Cox did admit these sixteen places in the entering class were *designated* for minorities, but they were not, nope, couldn't be, a quota, because that would be "an arbitrary limit on an unwanted minority by a group looking down its nose at them." One Supreme Court justice (unidentified on the recording) was quick to ask, "It did put a limit on the number of white people, didn't it?" which would seem to make it a quota of eighty-four people for whites, but Cox, after fumbling around at the obvious truth of that possibility, said the sixteen designated spots were for "qualified disadvantaged minority students," and glossed over the real question.

But let's look at his statement before proceeding. If these people were actually *qualified* in the same way that whites had to be qualified, why would affirmative action be necessary? And why *disadvantaged* students? What does family income or home address have to do with the matter? Certainly many poor white students of outstanding achievement had been admitted to exclusive schools over the years; was there a special onus on being disadvantaged and black so that lower scores and grades were necessary? And finally, what was a *minority?* Two generations of white students have seen the lie in that statement. Certainly Jews are a definable minority and so subject to discrimination that Hitler murdered them wholesale—not only are they not counted as a "minority" in this manner, they have often been discriminated against over the years for being too capable, to

---

[294] Why don't I use the politically correct term "African American"? Because there's no way to know they are all *American,* since many medical students apply from overseas, and it's highly unlikely they were all *African,* meaning from that continent. So "black" will have to serve. I would prefer not to slice up our population by skin tone at all, but that's what affirmative action does.

the extent that Ivy League schools once had quotas limiting how much of a class could be Jewish. Asians, particularly Japanese and Chinese, were subject to hideous discrimination in this country, but they also are almost *too* intelligent to be called a "minority" for the purposes of affirmative action. Hispanics, on the other hand, have suffered much *less* discrimination as a group than Jews or Asians because they did not come to this country in large numbers until after most discrimination was banned. America was a much less-Hispanic nation in the 1960s when the civil rights laws were passed. So why do Hispanics get special treatment? We often read of illegal immigrants who get into top colleges. If they are receiving preferential treatment in doing so, how does discrimination justify it, since these people came from places where almost everybody else was just like them and they suffered no discrimination at all? Keep in mind that in Mexico, Honduras, and Puerto Rico, being Hispanic doesn't qualify one for special treatment.

The real answer seems to be one so disgusting to the American mind that it is never actually expressed, but nothing else seems to fit the facts. Since liberals are the ones pushing for affirmative action in all cases, the explanation must lie with them, not conservatives who oppose it. The answer must be simply this: that *liberals actually believe blacks and Hispanics are not as intelligent as the rest of us*, and never will be.

There is simply no other explanation. If affirmative action is meant to make up for past discrimination, then it should be applied to the groups that were strongly discriminated against in this country for decades: blacks, Jews, and Asians. If affirmative action is only for the "well qualified," then there is no need for it at all. *No one* any longer claims that *qualified* minorities should not be accepted by colleges or hired by corporations. In fact, that fact gives the lie to liberal malarkey about "qualified minorities." After all, if they were as well qualified as the people they are hired/admitted in place of, there would be no complaints and no need for affirmative action.

So why do liberals constantly drone on about the need for it? It can only be that, when it comes to blacks and Hispanics, they believe there is absolutely no way that these people will be able to lift themselves to the intellectual level of other Americans, even given the past forty years of trying. And that can only mean that liberals believe, despite all the effort made to improve the education of minorities in the past forty years, that these minorities simply do not have the brainpower to make it without help from their liberal friends.

Again, I am against affirmative action and believe that rather than help, it has actively harmed the prospects of blacks and Hispanics in higher education. Just as one can't become stronger while walking with a crutch, these minorities are likely being harmed, not helped, by special rules that make their lives easier. But for those who continue to demand it, here are two questions: what is your rigorous definition of affirmative action, and why do you choose only two discriminated-against minorities for extra help?

The actual decision in *Bakke* is hardly a decision at all; instead it became a mashed-up combination of two five-to-four decisions—hardly the stuff of which longstanding government policy should be made. And yet, there you have it, an almost-accidental wrecking of thousands of planned careers of more-qualified candidates for jobs and college admissions that became hardened policy—policy that may have done much to damage America's productivity and innovation.

But back to *Bakke*. Justice Powell wrote the majority opinion, except that he was a majority of a single person. Look at this train-wreck of a decision, as announced in the opinion itself ("J." means "Justice," and "JJ." means "Justices"):

> POWELL, J., announced the Court's judgment and filed an opinion expressing his views of the case, in Parts I, III-A, and V-C of which WHITE, J., joined; and in Parts I and V-C of which BRENNAN, MARSHALL, and BLACKMUN, JJ., joined. BRENNAN, WHITE, MARSHALL, and BLACKMUN, JJ., filed an opinion concurring in the judgment in part and dissenting in part, post, p. 324. WHITE, J., post, p. 379, MARSHALL, J., post, p. 387, and BLACKMUN, J., post, p. 402, filed separate opinions. STEVENS, J., filed an opinion concurring in the judgment in part and dissenting in part, in which BURGER, C. J., and STEWART and REHNQUIST, JJ., joined, post, p. 408.[295]

Complicated as it seems, notice that while Justice Powell wrote the opinion, Justice White agrees only with three small parts of it, while Brennan, Blackmun, and Marshall agree only with two of those parts. Then those four write *another* opinion agreeing with part of the opinion and

---

[295] University of California Regents v. Bakke, 438 U.S. 265, 267–68 (1978).

disagreeing with another part. Then four *other* justices agree in part and disagree in part, but apparently just barely disagree enough *more* with the opinion to be called dissenters. On this pile of judicial garbage was built a policy that, at last decision, has at least twenty-five more years to run.[296]

The *Bakke* opinion lays out the camel's-nose-under-the-tent way that affirmative action grew to warp the entire admissions process at UC–Davis and every other selective university in the country. In 1973, the program didn't (openly) consider race, probably because administrators were thinking, mistakenly, that the Supreme Court would rule it unconstitutional for all the right reasons. Instead, applicants were "asked" if they wanted to be considered as "economically and/or educationally disadvantaged." Now think about this situation: this is a medical school making these decisions about people who will later make decisions that literally mean life or death for some patients, and it's willing to allow people to plead that they should be allowed in *because they got crappy educations*. That should make all of you planning surgery real happy. Affirmative action pimps would claim that, well, these people are just as *qualified* as the others (with admittedly crappy educations?) and after all, the grade system in medical school will sort out everyone who doesn't deserve to be there. Oh sure—after going to all this trouble to make the medical school class "look like America" and other liberal malarkey, they're going to flunk out all the minority students the first semester. No way, pal; once they've broken the old rules (education, preparation, capability) to let in people they've decided to favor, they'll keep breaking those rules until the final results match their beliefs, too. Justice Powell's opinion continues:

> No formal definition of "disadvantaged" was ever produced... but the chairman of the special committee screened each application to see whether it reflected economic or educational deprivation. Having passed this initial hurdle, the applications then were rated by the special committee in a fashion similar to that used by the general admissions committee, except that special candidates did not have to meet the 2.5 grade point average cut-off applied to regular applicants.[297]

---

[296] The preposterous Grutter v. Bollinger, 539 U.S. 306 (2003). We'll deal with this later, but I can't keep from mentioning Justice O'Connor's approval of an affirmative action program because it used race as part of a "highly individualized, holistic review of each applicant's file." The decision was apparently based on a highly individualized, holistic review of the Constitution, rather than actually, say, reading the words.

[297] *Bakke,* 438 U.S.at 274–75.

It was once a common gimmick of Communist governments to have a constitution that seemed to guarantee to their people all the rights we had in this country; the only problem was that no one but a handful of bosses actually got those rights. What few rights the chumps had and what they had to do to stay out of trouble were never actually *written down* anywhere; they were just supposed to guess at it. On the same lines, affirmative action was designed to choose certain "disadvantaged" people, *but there was no written definition of disadvantaged.* Ergo, they could choose certain racial groups and call them "disadvantaged" and ignore others, with no one able to point out their inconsistency. And if those "disadvantaged" were particularly thickheaded, the admissions committee was allowed to ignore its 2.5 GPA cutoff that applied to everyone else. That is equal to a B-minus or C-plus, or about an 80 percent average in undergraduate work. Ergo, the UC–Davis admissions committee was declaring it was going to allow some people into medical school who had done barely average in undergraduate classes, much less medical school. No problem; they knew who the good doctors were, since they worked at a medical school; it was all the middle-class chumps who were going to have to take their chances.

Interestingly, the "minority" admissions program only helped certain "minorities"—Justice Powell's opinion clearly shows that the affirmative action program boosted some and actually *damaged* the chances of others. He notes that from 1971 through 1974, "the special program resulted in the admission of 21 black students, 30 Mexican-Americans, and 12 Asians, for a total of 63 minority students."[298] Using the regular admissions criteria, the school would have admitted forty-four minority students, but only one would have been black and six would have been Mexican Americans. The rest—thirty-seven new medical students—would have been Asian. So not only did the program discriminate against whites, it also *discriminated against Asians*, screwing twenty-five of them out of admission to medical school. See what I mean about how liberals must actually think blacks and Hispanics are dumb? If they really are worried about *minorities*, why shaft the Asians?

It's not long before Powell is into the process of explaining that the laws of the United States don't allow what he wants, and then explaining that he's going to do it anyway and to hell with the law. He clearly quotes the appropriate law, which states, "No person in the United States shall, on

---

[298] *Id*, at 275.

the ground of race, color, or national origin, be excluded from participation in, be denied the benefits of, or be subjected to discrimination under any program or activity receiving Federal financial assistance."[299] And then he says that, well, he just doesn't give a rat's ass what the law says:

> The concept of "discrimination," like the phrase "equal protection of the laws," is susceptible of varying interpretations, for as Mr. Justice Holmes declared, "a word is not a crystal, transparent and unchanged, it is the skin of a living thought and may vary greatly in color and content according to the circumstances and the time in which it is used."[300]

What horseshit. If we are to believe this, then any judge on any federal court can make up anything he or she wants and it becomes law, despite what the Constitution might say. A word would mean what a judge says it does, and nothing more or less, to paraphrase Lewis Carroll. That leaves the rest of us to *guess* what the judges will decide the Constitution says on the next case. Sadly, that's how most liberals like it. No reason to worry about a real Constitution with real words meaning real things when the right number of Washington dinner parties and phony awards can convince a justice to change his or her mind the way those inside the Beltway wish.

Before it's all over, Powell has done the classic Orwellian trick of defining discrimination—special rights for certain citizens—as being *non*discrimination. He looks not into the Constitution or the law passed, but rather into what people involved with passing the law said at about the time the law was passed. He particularly likes what Senator Hubert Humphrey declared: "The bill has a simple purpose. That purpose is to give fellow citizens—Negroes—the same rights and opportunities that white people take for granted. This is no more than what was preached by the prophets, and by Christ Himself. It is no more than what our Constitution guarantees."[301] The lie here, of course, is that "the same rights and opportunities" would not give liberals what they wanted, because it would give minorities the same rights and opportunities to *fail* as the rest of the pop-

---

[299] *Id.* at 284.

[300] *Id.* at 284.

[301] *Id.* at 287. As a commentary on political correctness, note the use of the word "negroes," now considered heinous even to mention, and the use of the beliefs of Christ, something liberals would oppose mentioning in the twenty-first century.

ulation, something they disagreed with mightily. The entire concept of everyone in America having the same opportunity to be something (or not) was being stood on its head. It's as if the NBA were being told to fill at least one of every starting five with a white guy under 5'8" who couldn't jump, just to be "equal." After all, look at all those short guys who can't jump who would love to play professional basketball![302]

Of course, everyone had to make the obligatory bow to equal rights by saying, for example, "I yield to no one in my earnest hope that the time will come when an 'affirmative action' program is unnecessary and is, in truth, only a relic of the past. I would hope that we could reach this stage within a decade at the most. But the story of Brown v. Board of Education, decided almost a quarter of a century ago, suggests that that hope is a slim one."[303] But why was the hope a slim one? We aren't discussing a deadly virus but rather a judicial commandment that could be reversed. The best way to get rid of affirmative action would be to *get rid of affirmative action* and then carefully enforce laws against actual discrimination, but the court had no such faith in humanity, the United States, or the Constitution. It was going to end discrimination—by ensuring discrimination continued.

It was so clear that defending affirmative action as a constitutional right was impossible that Justice Powell has to admit it: "Preferring members of any one group for no reason other than race or ethnic origin is discrimination for its own sake. This the Constitution forbids."[304] And so Powell had to let Bakke into medical school, noting that the goal of preventing discrimination "does not justify a classification that imposes disadvantages upon persons like [Bakke], who bear no responsibility for whatever harm the beneficiaries of the special admissions program are thought to have suffered."[305] Just as every American with common sense would have told you, past discrimination cannot justify current discrimination.

But Powell can't let it just lie there, since that is so straightforward it would take future decisions out of the hands of liberal judges

---

[302] Even worse, true affirmative action would require that three or four of the starting five be nonathletic whites, since they are more than 60 percent of the population.

[303] *Bakke*, 438 U.S. at 403. This was Justice Blackmun getting his two cents' worth in. Note that the case has run an incredible 138 pages and we still haven't reached the dissent!

[304] *Id.* at 307.

[305] *Id.* at 310.

and university deans. So, how to phrase the matter in a way that would allow future mischief but still appear to be constitutional? Powell has to come up with a term so nebulous that opponents could never prove it existed, sort of like the way segregationists had used one simple book as a literacy test for whites and another much more complex book for blacks. So Powell decides it is permissible to work for "...the attainment of a diverse student body. This clearly is a constitutionally permissible goal for an institution of higher education. Academic freedom, *though not a specifically enumerated constitutional right*, long has been viewed as a special concern of the First Amendment. The freedom of a university to make its own judgments as to education includes the selection of its student body."[306] That seems admirable, but wait a minute. If a university is free to choose whom it wishes, why require it to take Bakke? And what is "diversity"? Again, it could mean anything a liberal wanted it to mean.[307] And I won't even go into the fact that Powell is saying that something not in the Constitution—"academic freedom"—is now a constitutional right.

The dissent points all this out, but it didn't matter. Justice Stevens notes that the lower court had correctly pointed out that Bakke would have been admitted to medical school *unless* there was discrimination to prevent it, and such discrimination violated not only the Title VI equal opportunity laws but also the Fourteenth Amendment and the California Constitution.[308] Stevens writes that there's no need to use the Constitution to decide this case, since the Equal Opportunity Act clearly states such discrimination is illegal. Even better, he says, going back to the days when the civil rights laws were written, that the idea of discrimination in *favor* of minorities was only brought up by *opponents* of the law who feared it would be used *in exactly the way the court was now using it*. In answer, the same Senator Humphrey so proudly quoted in the majority decision had said:

---

[306] *Id.* at 311–12. (Italics mine, but I wanted show how Powell simply ignored the Constitution and did what he and liberals wanted).

[307] Or nothing at all. By 2007, Kansas University was proclaiming it loved diversity because "diversity matters at the University of Kansas. It matters because diversity enriches our ability to solve problems and create new knowledge. It is our goal to have the richest possible mix of perspectives, life-experiences, interests, world-views and cultures in our campus community." Which means absolutely nothing, but you can read it yourself at http://www.diversity.ku.edu/ and similar tripe at hundreds of other college websites.

[308] *Bakke,* 438 U.S. at 409. This is an actual time when the Fourteenth Amendment was used properly by the court.

> The answer to this question [what was meant by "discrimination"] is that if race is not a factor, we do not have to worry about discrimination because of race...The Internal Revenue Code does not provide that colored people do not have to pay taxes, or that they can pay their taxes 6 months later than everyone else.[309]

But indeed, the Supreme Court has now said something tantamount to allowing "colored people"[310] to pay their taxes later than everyone else by stating clearly that some minorities don't have to meet the same standards as everyone else, and the standards they must meet are substantially lower than everyone else's. Ah well, what's the problem? It's not as if anyone's *life* was going to hang in the balance later by having an unqualified doctor work on them.

Bakke's preposterous shifting sand of legality became the bedrock for another generation of court decisions, and then went even farther in a moronic decision written by Justice Sandra O'Connor in 2003, not long before her well-deserved retirement. This time it wasn't a white male from California getting the shaft, but rather a white female from Michigan. *The New York Times* was so excited, it journalistically peed down its leg: "The Supreme Court preserved affirmative action in university admissions today by a one-vote margin but with a forceful endorsement of the role of racial diversity on campus in achieving a more equal society."[311] "Preserved" is what you say if you favor the action; "extended" would be more semantically neutral. "Forceful endorsement" means you *really* like what they did, and throwing in the liberal buzzwords of "racial diversity" and "more equal society" shows further approval. For a liberal, "more equal society" is always a good thing. But would a "more equal society" be good if it meant we all had to have our legs hacked off to be exactly the height of the shortest person in America?

Grutter v. Michigan[312] seemed to present the same situation as *Bakke*, with a white plaintiff suing a university for discrimination. Barbara Grutter had completed her undergraduate work with a 3.8 grade-point average, and scored 161 on the Law School Admissions Test (LSAT). But that performance wasn't a lock for the University of Michigan, whose law school was often rated in the top ten nationwide. Her GPA was higher than the average entrant,

---

[309] *Id.* at 413 (quoting 110 Cong. Rec. 5864 [1964]).

[310] Hey, don't blame me—it was the liberals' own Hubert Humphrey who used the term.

[311] Linda Greenhouse, "The Supreme Court: Affirmative Action; Justice Back Affirmative Action by 5 to 4, but Wider Vote Bans a Racial Point System," *New York Times*, June 24, 2003.

[312] 539 U.S. 306 (2003).

but that LSAT score would put her in the bottom quarter of the admitted class. Grutter was turned down. Still, she knew her score was better than *some* people admitted to the school (many of whom were minority students or various sorts of preferred-status types) so she sued, charging discrimination.

The district federal court, knowing discrimination when it saw it, ruled that she was indeed a victim of such and ordered her admitted. The University of Michigan wasn't going to take yes for an answer, so it appealed. By the time the case reached the Supreme Court twenty-five years after *Bakke*, the diversity scam had become so entrenched in the thinking of liberal America that the list of groups filing friend of the court briefs filled almost five pages of the decision—including the American Bar Association, American Psychological Association, attorneys general for eighteen states, the Mexican American Legal Defense and Education Fund, the city of Philadelphia, Harvard University, and even Exxon-Mobil, doubtless trying to uphold the diversity plan it had in place since *Bakke* to avoid lawsuits by all the qualified people it *hadn't* hired in two decades.

Sandra O'Connor, probably considering herself an affirmative-action baby as the first female on the Supreme Court, was eager to continue the mess that *Bakke* had been, and did so by defining crap as cactus blossoms. She begins by quoting the Michigan Law School admission policy, which looked for "individuals with a substantial promise of success in law school" and "a strong likelihood of succeeding in the practice of law."[313] That seems admirable, since they were, after all, running a law school. But it's what followed that last phrase that threw in the monkey wrench, since the sentence read "a strong likelihood of succeeding in the practice of law *and contributing in diverse ways to the well-being of others.*" Like so many other politically correct statements, it seemed to mean something without meaning anything. For example, a squad of all-white nurses could contribute in various different ways to the well-being of others, probably better than a bunch of liberal law students of carefully chosen colors. But the term "diverse" was not meant that way, but rather in that squishy new-age way that means something about different ethnic groups without specifying which ones or how many or what the advantages are exactly to having lawyers with different levels of melanin in their skins. In order to stay nebulous, the policy lapses into the jargon of academic bureaucracy: "The hallmark of that policy is its focus on academic ability coupled with a flexible assessment of

---

[313] Grutter v. Bollinger et al., 539 U.S. 306, 313–14 (2003).

applicants' talents, experiences, and potential 'to contribute to the learning of those around them.'"[314] OK, they *have* to say "academic ability," since they are (supposedly) in the academic profession, but what are the talents and experiences needed? Well, that standard is "flexible." Then what does it mean to "contribute to the learning of those around them"? Are minority students supposed to tutor the whites? Does seeing a darker person somehow help a white student learn better? It's difficult to prove any real advantages to "diversity" in a student body, since diversity itself cannot be defined without setting off all those nondiscrimination alarms in the Equal Opportunity Act. Defining diversity would mean setting out quotas for each racial and ethnic group, and the court had to admit in *Bakke* that was not a good thing to do so. Instead, it left the country with a vague proposition that an employer or university could accept anyone it wanted so long as it wasn't a quota system, so long as they let in some minorities who weren't particularly well qualified[315] but not too many, said amount not being defined because, after all, that would be illegal. And of course, the company or university could be sued no matter what it did, making it a wonderful employment opportunity for liberal lawyers. To give you an idea of how it sounds in practice, here's more of what the Michigan Law School policy stated: "The policy does not restrict the types of diversity contributions eligible for 'substantial weight' in the admissions process, but instead recognizes 'many possible bases for diversity admissions.'"[316] That is, we can make this stuff up as we go along and you can't hold us responsible for it and you can't even predict what we might decide is "diverse," although being a one-eyed Eskimo raised by walruses may be almost as good as being the child of black professors.

So how did Justice O'Connor deal with this? The way liberals always do, which is by floating a bunch of malarkey on the waters and hoping nobody questions it too specifically for fear of being called a racist. O'Connor had to note that the admissions director for the Michigan Law School did, well, *keep track* of how many minority students were being considered for the school, but that was only to make sure a "critical mass" of minority students would

---

[314] *Id.* at 315.

[315] Let me state again for the record that the whole idea of *affirmative* action is to admit and hire people who *do not come up to the usual hiring standards*. No one has ever argued that minorities who *do* meet the standards should be turned down (until affirmative action, which itself in a nonquota sort of way cheated thousands of Asians out of jobs and positions in college, but liberals decided that's not their problem).

[316] *Grutter*, 539 U.S. at 316.

be attending the school.[317] But never let it be said that a "critical mass" meant anything specific, since the admissions director stressed "that he did not seek to admit any particular number or percentage of underrepresented minority students." See, we want to make sure we admit "underrepresented minorities" (meaning not Asians, because they're too smart), and we want to admit a "critical mass" of them, *but that doesn't mean we're actually counting how many we let in.* In the days before political correctness, this sort of swill wouldn't have made a passing mark in an eighth-grade book report; nowadays we swallow it whole for fear someone might see us questioning it and denounce us as racist or, even worse, in favor of global warming.

So how to explain it? Since things this irrational can't be explained, O'Connor simply passes the buck back to the just-barely five-to-four decision in *Bakke*[318] and says that, well, Justice Powell said diversity was a compelling governmental interest as long as the program was narrowly tailored not to blah, blah, blah, and adds, "The guarantee of equal protection cannot mean one thing when applied to one individual and something else when applied to a person of another color. If both are not accorded the same protection, then it is not equal." Which means—nothing. It certainly doesn't mean that the same *standards* should be applied to all students; that is just what "diversity" is supposed to *prevent.* In fact, *inequality* is exactly what "diversity" was all about, despite its high-flying prose. The idea is to admit most students according to one set of standards, then set another, lower set of standards for melanin-rich students.

O'Connor continues in that vein, pointing out all the ways the laws of our great nation *don't* allow discrimination and then finally saying, well, we're going to discriminate anyway. For instance, she notes "governmental action based on race—a *group* classification long recognized as in most circumstances irrelevant and therefore prohibited—should be subjected to detailed judicial inquiry." The use of race to make decisions "must be analyzed by a reviewing court under strict scrutiny...such classifications are constitutional only if they are narrowly tailored to further compelling governmental interests." And she quotes Justice Powell's *Bakke* decision with, "'It is not an interest in simple ethnic diversity, in which a specified

---

[317] "Critical mass" is a physics term originally used to state how much fissionable material was needed to set off a nuclear reaction, and the thought of a certain number of minority law students coming together and exploding would seem undesirable, but who am I to question diversity?

[318] "The decision produced six separate opinions, none of which commanded a majority of the Court." *Grutter*, 539 U.S. at 322.

percentage of the student body is in effect guaranteed to be members of selected ethnic groups,' that can justify the use of race."

So what can jump all these hoops and survive the government's "strict scrutiny" and still be constitutional by not preferring one race over another race, or any quota at all? Why look, kids, it's *diversity*, which Justice Powell said was a "compelling state interest" without ever actually saying what diversity was because—that would be unconstitutional. And to justify this diversity scam? Justice O'Connor tries to take cover by writing, "In announcing the principle of student body diversity as a compelling state interest, Justice Powell invoked our cases recognizing a constitutional dimension, grounded in the First Amendment, of educational autonomy: 'The freedom of a university to make its own judgments as to education includes the selection of its student body.'" If you read it, the First Amendment doesn't actually say anything about schools, but shut up.

Yeah, that's it—you see, universities have some freedom *above and beyond that of mere citizens* to discriminate in order to make us better people. If a mere citizen tried this stuff, he'd be drawn and quartered, but "educational autonomy" makes it legal. Oh yes—you in the back—a question? Wouldn't the universities have had this educational autonomy in the 1950s, when some thought allowing only white students admission was part of their educational freedom? Oh, don't be ridiculous. They've always had freedom—to do what we want them to do, and in the 1950s we wanted them not to have any freedom.

O'Connor goes on the warpath—oops, I mean, gets very enthusiastic—over the entire issue of diversity, by noting that the armed forces and large corporations are all convinced it does them worlds of good. Without any hard facts, of course, since no one is ever allowed to define "diversity" exactly, because just doing so would be unconstitutionally racist. But trust us, folks, it works and it's good! And she finally comes to the conclusion that all prodiversity goons must reach—that diversity is good because it *does the opposite* of what we claim it does. Try this statement: "In order to cultivate a set of leaders with legitimacy in the eyes of the citizenry, it is necessary that the path to leadership be visibly open to talented and qualified individuals of every race and ethnicity."[319] Sounds great, but what she really is saying is that in order to give our leaders legitimacy, we must *close off* the path to leadership to one in eight clearly qualified whites so

---

[319] *Grutter*, 539 U.S. at 332.

that talented but admittedly less-qualified individuals of some, but not all, other races and ethnicities can be admitted. After all, her own opinion notes that, in the absence of "diversity," only 4 percent of qualified admitted students would be minorities, but with the added nudge, 14.5 percent got in.[320] That means a percentage of the applicants equal to 10.5 percent of those admitted got turned down because they weren't the right color, since they were obviously *more* qualified than those admitted in their place. The ugly truth about "diversity" is that it opens up doors to somewhat less-qualified applicants only by shutting the doors in the faces of somewhat *more*-qualified applicants.

Still don't believe me? At the end of her majority opinion, Justice O'Connor notes that it had been twenty-five years since the court first approved using race to "further an interest in student body diversity. Since that time, the number of minority applicants with high grades and test scores has indeed increased. We expect that 25 years from now, the use of racial preferences will no longer be necessary to further the interest approved today."[321] She of course makes no attempt to correlate "diversity" with these improved test scores, nor offer any hard evidence of higher scores; she just states the sad fact that clearly superior candidates have been turned down for twenty-five years in the name of political correctness and that yet another generation will get the same treatment.

So why should I complain? After all, haven't a lot of white students gotten special treatment over the years? Certainly. One of my best friends as an undergraduate[322] was a guy whose father was dean of the law school at, yes, the University of Michigan. Not surprisingly, this friend went to the University of Michigan Law School after graduating. Perhaps he got a little "extra nudge" to do so; I don't know. But the difference between this and "diversity" is that *no one made a Supreme Court decision that he had to be let in and everyone like him had to be let in ad infinitum.* Perhaps the next dean's son wouldn't make it or wouldn't prefer law; perhaps the next dean had no son; but there was never the heavy hand of the federal government requiring nepotism. "Diversity," on the other hand, is enforced by a gun in the hand of every federal officer, although there are no real standards for what it means. Perhaps someday we'll find there are hard facts justifying

---

[320] *Id.* at 321, referring to the Michigan Law School's class admitted in 2000.

[321] *Id.* at 343.

[322] Greg Smith, Princeton '68.

"diversity" without being hard enough facts to show that "diversity" is actually illegal discrimination. But today it's enforced whether it's good or not, simply because five unelected officials once said so.

WE SAID YOU HAD FREE SPEECH, SO SHUT UP
HILL V. COLORADO (2000)

Roe v. Wade wasn't the court's last act of magnificent arrogance over abortion. Take the "free speech" issue it visited in *Hill v. Colorado*, in the year 2000. The problem for the court and liberals was that pro-lifers were lining up outside hospitals and abortion clinics and trying to get the women walking in to rethink their abortion plans. Justice John Paul Stevens had no trouble seeing as constitutional a Colorado law[323] keeping the protestors one hundred feet from the entrance to any health-care facility, but explaining why it was constitutional was a lot tougher. One of the problems was the court's decision in *Schenck* v. *Pro-Choice Network of Western N.Y.*[324] three years earlier. A judge facing the police's insistence that they could not deal with the problem of abortion protestors properly[325] issued a temporary restraining order that "enjoined defendants from physically blockading the clinics, physically abusing or tortiously[326] harassing anyone entering

---

[323] Colo. Rev. Stat. § 18-9-122(3) (1999).

[324] 519 U.S. 357 (1997).

[325] "The protests were constant, overwhelming police resources; when the police arrived, the protesters simply dispersed and returned later; prosecution of arrested protesters was difficult because patients were often reluctant to cooperate for fear of making their identity public; and those who were convicted were not deterred from returning to engage in unlawful conduct." Schenck v. Pro-Choice Network of Western N.Y., 519 U.S. 357, 363–64 (1997). Thank God they don't give up that easily when facing real criminals such as burglars and murderers.

[326] Acting in a manner that would cause a tort, which is a legal wrong.

131

or leaving the clinics, and "demonstrating within 15 feet of any person" entering or leaving the clinics.[327] The Supreme Court agreed to take up the matter and decided that it was acceptable to declare a fixed area around the clinics forbidden to the protestors, but the idea of a "floating buffer zone" could not be constitutional.[328] This opinion, written by Chief Justice Rehnquist, seemed reasonable at the time, since the First Amendment is generally considered to be the most precious of the Bill of Rights and includes all that stuff about speech and protesting.

But apparently the right to abortion is even more precious. In 2000, Justice John Paul Stevens had to explain away this case and the First Amendment. As so many Supreme Court cases that blindside the public do, he begins by admitting that he has no right to do what he is about to do, and he admits it in three ways:

> The First Amendment interests of petitioners are clear and undisputed. As a preface to their legal challenge, petitioners emphasize three propositions. *First*, they accurately explain that the areas protected by the statute encompass all the public ways within 100 feet of every entrance to every health care facility everywhere in the State of Colorado...*Second*, they correctly state that their leafleting, sign displays, and oral communications are protected by the First Amendment. The fact that the messages conveyed by those communications may be offensive to their recipients does not deprive them of constitutional protection. *Third*, the public sidewalks, streets, and ways affected by the statute are "quintessential" public forums for free speech[329] (italics added).

So, case closed, eh? After all, this is the Supreme Court that decided that exotic dancing was "speech" under the law[330] and said in 1971 that "Fuck the Draft" crudely lettered on a jacket was free speech[331] and had to be protected because of the First Amendment; surely this settles the matter. Uhhhhh... no. This is all just telegraphing the punch that is about to be slammed into

---

[327] *Schenck,* 519 U.S. at 364.

[328] *Id.* at 361.

[329] Hill et al. v. Colorado, 530 U.S. 703, 714-15 (2000).

[330] City of Erie v. Pap's A.M., 120 S. Ct. 1382 (2000).

[331] Cohen v. California, 403 U.S. 15 (1971).

the gut of the freedom-of-speech guarantee. After all that, Justice Stevens notes, "On the other hand, petitioners do not challenge the legitimacy of the state interests that the statute is intended to serve. It is a traditional exercise of the States' 'police powers to protect the health and safety of their citizens.'"[332] See? After telling everyone that they simply should have averted their eyes if they thought they might be offended by "Fuck the Draft" on the back of a hippie's jacket, the court is now highly concerned with the health of its citizens subjected to free speech. Why, it might injure the little dears to have to listen to someone who disagrees with them! Contrast this to what the court says in *Cohen v. California* about using the f-word in public:

> The constitutional right of free expression is powerful medicine in a society as diverse and populous as ours. It is *designed and intended to remove governmental restraints from the arena of public discussion*, putting the decision as to what views shall be voiced largely into the hands of each of us[333] (italics added).

Yep, no way your government is going to interfere with those speech rights, pal. Can't be done. Wouldn't be prudent. Unless, that is, you're opposed to abortion. Then you have to understand that "it is a traditional exercise of the States' 'police powers to protect the health and safety of their citizens.'"[334] Now, you might be thinking that it's the abortion *protestors* who are trying to protect the health and safety of fellow citizens by talking them out of abortions, but put that out of your mind. They're actually trying to *damage* the health and safety of clinic workers and customers, and so they must be stopped. After all, "the unwilling listener's interest in avoiding unwanted communication has been repeatedly identified in our cases. It is an aspect of the broader 'right to be let alone' that one of our wisest Justices characterized as 'the most comprehensive of rights and the right most valued by civilized men.'"[335]

---

[332] *Id.* at 215.

[333] *Id.* at 24.

[334] *Hill*, 530 U.S. at 715. Even better, this quote about protecting the health and safety of the citizens comes from a case involving the safety of implanted pacemakers and has nothing to do with freedom of speech, which shows that, once they've got a majority, justices simply cut things out of previous cases and paste them together—sort of like a kidnaper does with a ransom note.

[335] *Id.* at 716–17. He is quoting Justice Brandeis's dissent in Olmstead v. United States, 277 U. S. 438, 478 (1928), which means the court majority *didn't* agree with Brandeis on this.

Ergo, you have a supreme right to be left alone if you want an abortion, but have no right to be left alone if you're just trying to go about your daily business and someone wants to fuck the draft.

If you don't believe my view of this, try the dissent's version in *Hill v. Colorado*:

> What is before us, after all, is a speech regulation directed against the opponents of abortion, and it therefore enjoys the benefit of the "ad hoc nullification machine" that the Court has set in motion to push aside whatever doctrines of constitutional law stand in the way of that *highly favored practice*[336] (italics added).

> A speaker wishing to approach another for the purpose of communicating *any* message except one of protest, education, or counseling may do so without first securing the other's consent. Whether a speaker must obtain permission before approaching within eight feet—and whether he will be sent to prison for failing to do so—depends entirely on *what he intends to say* when he gets there[337] (italics added).

> Just three Terms ago, in upholding an injunction against antiabortion activities, the Court refused to rely on any supposed "right of the people approaching and entering the facilities to be left alone." *Schenck* v. *Pro-Choice Network of Western N.Y.*, 519 U. S. 357, 383 (1997). It expressed "doubt" that this "right... accurately reflects our First Amendment jurisprudence." Finding itself in something of a jam...the Court today neatly repackages the repudiated "right" as an "interest" the State may decide to protect, and then places it onto the scales opposite the right to free speech in a traditional public forum.[338]

It's so clear that the majority has decided it wants what it wants when it wants it (and here it wants abortion protestors to shut up) that it's willing

---

[336] *Hill*, 530 U.S. at 741 (2000).

[337] *Id.* at 742. Minor citations dropped.

[338] *Id.* at 750–51.

to ignore not only the Constitution, but its own decisions from as recently as three years before! The dissent, written by that Beelzebub of liberals, Justice Scalia, does what Scalia does so well, which is skewer those who think they can cut and fit the Constitution to match their politics. Since any restriction on speech is supposed to be "narrowly tailored," according to the court's previous decisions, Scalia takes aim at the majority's pretensions:

> And if...forbidding peaceful, nonthreatening, but uninvited speech from a distance closer than eight feet is a "narrowly tailored" means of preventing the obstruction of entrance to medical facilities (the governmental interest the State asserts), narrow tailoring must refer not to the standards of Versace, but to those of Omar the tentmaker.[339]

Like most dictators, liberals in the United States do not find humor in anything they do. It's all so serious, so crucial. We must protect women's right to abortion, the environment, gay rights, polar bears, recycling, recycling gay polar bears, and all those other things so serious that laughter is banned, especially if aimed at them. But the truth is, any dictatorship remains so only by ruthlessly squelching all dissent, and humor is the worst of all, since dictators cannot tolerate being laughed at. Once again, the liberals on the court got what they wanted, and what they wanted was to make abortion easy, cheap, common, and undamaging to the psyches of the women who decided to get it. As to the damage to the would-be future citizens of the United States, well, that's OK.

---

[339] *Id.* at 749.

WHAT'S MINE IS MINE, AND OH, YEAH—WHAT'S YOURS IS MINE, TOO *KELO V. CITY OF NEW LONDON (2005)*

When a real estate developer needs a piece of property owned by several other people, how does he get his hands on it? He has to go to each person, keeping quiet about his ultimate goal, and buy each piece of property separately. If someone sells cheaply and someone holds out for much more, he pays them and averages out the cost, not worrying about someone who might feel cheated or someone else who feels smug for hitting it big.

But what happens when a governmental unit needs property? Couldn't they just negotiate with the owners and pay the price they finally agree on? Well, they could, but come on, they're the *government*—why should they have to play by everyone else's rules? After all, governments don't pay *taxes* or anything stupid like that, so why pay actual market price for a piece of property? Needless to say, governments thought of this scam a long time ago. It's called eminent domain, "the inherent power of a governmental entity to take privately owned property, especially land, and convert it to public use, subject to reasonable compensation for the taking."[340] Except the "reasonable compensation" is hardly ever reasonable; after all, if the government paid what the property was worth, why bother to have eminent

---

[340] *Black's Law Dictionary, Eighth Edition.*

domain?[341] And "public use" is a very elastic term, especially following the Supreme Court's decision in *Kelo v. City of New London*.[342]

Unlike many power grabs by the Supreme Court, eminent domain is actually mentioned in the Bill of Rights, in the Fifth Amendment. After all that stuff about not-testifying-on-the-grounds-it-may-incriminate-me and due process, it winds up with "nor shall private property be taken for public use without just compensation." Lawyers call it the Takings Clause. Most arguments over the years have been over whether a person received a particularly low price for their property; generally, the answer is that if the government gives you pennies on the dollar, there's not much you can do. There's even a famous case, *Penn Central Transportation v. New York City*,[343] in which the owners of the famed Grand Central Terminal[344] in Manhattan were told they could not build an office tower atop the terminal. Penn Central claimed that amounted to a taking of private property, since it would likely cause them to lose tens of millions of dollars in property value if they were not allowed to use their own property interest—that is, the air space above their own land.

Piffle, said the Supreme Court (through Justice Brennan's opinion). The city's Landmarks Preservation Commission didn't actually *take* property away from Penn Central; it only blocked its use. Showing that they had been denied the chance "to exploit a property interest they…had believed was available for development is simply quite untenable."[345] After all, Justice Brennan notes, many decisions by higher courts "uniformly reject the proposition that diminution in property value, standing alone, can establish a 'taking.'"[346] So just because your property is worth a few dozen million less because of an unelected board's vote, that's not a "taking," and the government doesn't owe you a nickel.

Even worse, Justice Brennan then admits that the Supreme Court, after 190 years, still doesn't know what the hell it's doing in such cases. "The

---

[341] Allow me to explain the economics involved: if the government is willing to pay the actual market value for the properties it wants, it can just pay up, as private developers do. The only reason eminent domain needs to be used is if the government wants to pay *less than the market value* and shaft some poor schmuck.

[342] 545 U.S. 469 (2005).

[343] 438 U.S. 104 (1978).

[344] Well, it used to be the most famous railroad station in the United States, the terminus of the New York Central Railway and at one time the setting for an anthology radio series. Nowadays, who knows from railroad stations and radio shows?

[345] Penn Central Transportation Co. v. New York City, 438 U.S. 104, 130 (1978).

[346] *Id.* at 131.

question of what constitutes a 'taking' for purposes of the Fifth Amendment has proved to be a problem of considerable difficulty...this Court, quite simply, has been unable to develop any 'set formula' for determining when 'justice and fairness' require that economic injuries caused by public action be compensated by the government, rather than remain disproportionately concentrated on a few persons. Indeed, we have frequently observed that whether a particular restriction will be rendered invalid by the government's failure to pay for any losses proximately caused by it depends largely 'upon the particular circumstances [in that] case.'"[347] Translation: We just make this stuff up as we go along.

In several areas of judicial rulemaking, the Rehnquist court had cut back on some of the worst excesses of the Warren (1953–69) and Burger (1969–86) eras, but the arrogance of the federal government toward the citizens who supposedly ruled it kept growing. In 2005, it reached a high-water mark in *Kelo v. City of New London*,[348] and angered millions of people because it struck right at the heart of the American dream, taking away people's private residences for someone else's private development.

Before going into the specifics of the case, let's examine the premises used in such situations: a city or state has an area that has become rundown over the years and comes up with (or is more likely convinced by a developer to accept) a plan to reverse the decline. We've all heard of such plans, funded by millions in government grants, loans, or loan guarantees, usually with huge tax abatements thrown in. These seem like good ideas at first, but consider this: Why did the area become rundown? Who was in charge when the area fell apart and employers fled? The same governmental entities that now claim they have the answer to the problem! To which private citizens should ask, why the hell should we trust you? How many thousands of times in recent years have governments spent billions in tax money on projects that don't improve anything and occasionally make things even *worse?* Huge housing projects such as the infamous Cabrini Green in Chicago replaced thousands of privately owned homes and businesses in minority areas in the 1950s and '60s—areas that at the time were called "slums." The housing projects ended up being owned by no one and cared for by no one, greatly worsening the so-called "urban blight" that planners said they were going to improve, with the added injury of cheating

---

[347] *Id.* at 123–24.

[348] 545 U.S. 469 (2005).

many homeowners and businesspeople out of their hard-earned property. What had been a poor area (in income) soon became a Martian landscape of crime and decay, all thanks to city planners. But of course, governments are never discouraged by their failures; they are simply energized to try *another* hugely expensive pipe dream at even higher cost to the taxpayers.

Another giant irony is the tax abatements offered by governments to employers or developers in order to improve their "tax base." Cities, states, and school districts give businesses ten-to-fifty years of freedom from taxes or lower rates in order to encourage these businesses to set up in their areas. More recently, governmental groups have set up special districts where the businesses or developers *actually get to collect and use* the taxes paid by individuals in their areas. The idea is that the money raised will be used to improve services in the area, but in practice there's no guarantee. Of course, when offering these tax abatements, governments don't actually cut their *spending*, so who ends up footing the bill for these huge developments? The individual taxpayers already in the area, who are burdened by the high taxes and rundown condition caused by the government itself! So, with that background, let's look at what the Supreme Court did to private property rights in *Kelo*. Here's the first paragraph of the opinion by Justice John Paul Stevens, with my comments in brackets:

> The city of New London (hereinafter City) sits at the junction of the Thames River and the Long Island Sound in southeastern Connecticut. Decades of economic decline [*either caused by or ignored by the government*] led a state agency in 1990 to designate the City a "distressed municipality" [*who allowed it to become distressed?*]. In 1996, the Federal Government closed the Naval Undersea Warfare Center, which had been located in the Fort Trumbull area of the City and had employed over 1,500 people [*your government at work!*]. In 1998, the City's unemployment rate was nearly double that of the state, and its population of just under 24,000 residents was at its lowest since 1920 [*thanks to decades of corruption and discouragement of private investment because of high taxes*].[349]

Another question you should ask about this is why an area becomes distressed when the federal government closes a longtime military center.

---

349 Kelo v. City of New London, 545 U.S. 469 (2005).

Look at California's Silicon Valley, where computer companies are constantly spawning new companies as their highly capable employees go off to begin new enterprises. Xerox's influence may decline, but Cisco and Apple and others replace that and grow even larger. On the other hand, government employment seems to deaden people's interest in making the world a better place and themselves richer—few startup companies appear around government emplacements; instead, people just sit around and wait for their tax-supported paychecks, and when the government shuts down a location, usually years after its usefulness has ended, *more* government checks are needed to support the former employees.

So along comes a private developer looking to enrich himself at the expense of the "distressed municipality." He talks various government officials into making him the official developer and condemning the property he wants to use. In this particular case, it included the former Fort Trumbull and 115 privately owned properties, most of them with wonderful views of Long Island Sound. If the developer had tried to assemble this property himself, it would have taken years and cost millions, putting the profitability of his plans in doubt. It's much easier to get various governments to bitch-slap the private property owners into giving up their land and homes at discount prices so he can make big profits. (Although the New London Development Corporation was officially nonprofit, there was plenty of profit to be made from the deal itself and the buildings that would be built.) "We the people," indeed!

The victims of this plot were not exactly unsympathetic profit-mongers. Susette Kelo had bought her home in 1997 and had "made extensive improvements to her house, which she prizes for its water view." Another plaintiff in the original case, Wilhelmina Dery, "was born in her Fort Trumbull house in 1918 and has lived there her entire life," along with her husband, who married her sixty years before the case same to court. In all, nine plaintiffs held fifteen properties being condemned, with ten of them occupied by the owner or a family member. As Justice Stevens had to admit, "There is no allegation that any of these properties is blighted or otherwise in poor condition; rather, they were condemned only because they happen to be located in the development area."[350]

What to do, what to do? Hmmm. Justice Stevens sets up the land grab by stating, "Two polar propositions are perfectly clear. On the one hand, it

---

[350] *Id.* at 469.

has long been accepted that the sovereign may not take the property of *A* for the sole purpose of transferring it to another private party *B*, even though *A* is paid just compensation."[351] True enough. So why do I get the feeling that *A* is about to get screwed? Stevens continues: "On the other hand, it is equally clear that a state may transfer property from one private party to another if future 'use by the public' is the purpose of the taking." But then, he has to admit, this is not going to happen. The New London City Hall is not going to be built there, nor will the land be turned into a public park. This will clearly be a private area of new offices, retail businesses, and condos. Justice Stevens adds that "while many state courts in the mid-19th century endorsed 'use by the public' as the proper definition of public use, that narrow view steadily eroded over time. Not only was the 'use by the public' test difficult to administer...but it proved to be impractical given the diverse and always evolving needs of society." Translation: government always gets what it wants, and it always wants more, and many judges are ready to give privately owned property to do it, usually at great cost to the owners. I love phrases like "the diverse and always evolving needs to society." So apparently high-minded, yet so hard to pin down, leaving it useful for a wide spectrum of ways to shaft the public out of its property and money. Justice Stevens goes on, noting that "[t]he disposition of this case therefore turns on the question whether the City's development plan serves a 'public purpose.' Without exception, our cases have defined that concept broadly, reflecting our longstanding policy of deference to legislative judgments in this field." Translation: if another governmental entity ("legislative judgments") wants to screw citizens out of their hard-earned property, we almost always ("longstanding policy") let them do it, whatever the actual law says ("our cases have defined that concept broadly"). Stevens then cites a decision made by an even more liberal Supreme Court in 1984, *Hawaii Housing Authority v. Midkiff*,[352] in which a socialistic state government literally took away property from its owners and handed it over to people who had been leasing the land for many years, claiming some sort of racial justice by reducing the "concentration of land ownership." Even the normally wacko-leftist Ninth Circuit Court of Appeals turned down that idea, but the Supreme Court was ready to go for anything, even Leninist

---

[351] *Id.*

[352] 467 U. S. 229 (1984).

ideas of land redistribution, overturning the lower court's decision.[353] Then Stevens says the "petitioners" (that is, the poor New London landowners) "urge us to adopt a new bright-line rule[354] that economic development does not qualify as a public use." They also hope that the court will (sensibly) rule that "using eminent domain for economic development impermissibly blurs the boundary between public and private takings." Not a chance, pal. In addition, "just as we decline to second-guess the City's considered judgments about the efficacy of its development plan, we also decline to second-guess the City's determinations as to what lands it needs to acquire in order to effectuate the project." As one government entity to another, do whatever the hell you want to the citizens and private property, and we'll back you up. As Stevens reaches the end of his opinion, clearly allowing the state and local governments to use eminent domain in any way they wish, he adds a hilarious note: "nothing in our opinion precludes any State from placing further restrictions on its exercise of the takings power." That is, if states want to hold themselves back from taking anything and everything they want, we won't stop them—as if the real problem in public life is forcing states to use *more* power, not less. Still, *Kelo* angered so many people that states did feel compelled to pass laws making it clear where the boundaries were in shafting their own taxpayers. Among others, the state of Texas did, with a couple of exceptions, one of them being "the [Dallas] Cowboys' construction plans for a new $650 million stadium."[355] The Texas legislature tends to be biased toward private property interests until football gets in the way. That stadium ended up costing more than a billion dollars.

Justice Sandra O'Connor, that waffling, liberal-conservative mugwump, managed to be offended enough by this decision that she wrote the dissent, joined by more reliable conservatives Rehnquist, Scalia, and Thomas. Early on she states, "When interpreting the Constitution, we begin with the unremarkable presumption that every word in the document has independent meaning, 'that no word was unnecessarily used, or needlessly added.'"[356] Of course, considering the Supreme Court's increas-

---

[353] In *Midkiff*, the court noted that just seventy-two landowners held 47 percent of the land in Hawaii, so the state felt it should be broken up. Of course, they conveniently ignored the fact that just *two* landowners, the state and federal governments, owned 49 *percent* of the land—something they didn't feel the need to change.

[354] A "bright-line rule" is one that courts make that actually allows people to understand what the hell is being decided: if A occurs, then B is legal and C is illegal. Courts hate doing this because it removes so many opportunities for judicial mischief. Here, Stevens clearly doesn't want to do that.

[355] "The Cowboys Take the Field," *Time*, September 11, 2005.

[356] *Kelo*, 545 U.S. 429 (quoting Wright v. United States, 302 U. S. 583, 588 [1938]).

ing latitude in deciding what was "constitutional" in the past seventy years, such a presumption was anything but *un*remarkable. Her big problem, though, is separating the truly stinky decision in *Midkiff* from the even-stinkier *Kelo.* To do so, she slices and dices the "public use" section of the Fifth Amendment, saying that in *Midkiff,* at least, the "extraordinary, precondemnation use of the targeted property inflicted affirmative harm on society."[357] Whereas in New London, the city and state can't say private homeowners are damaging society, rather that, well, maybe things would be *better* for the area if the new development were made. If that's the case, O'Connor says, "the specter of condemnation hangs over all property. Nothing is to prevent the State from replacing any Motel 6 with a Ritz-Carlton, any home with a shopping mall, or any farm with a factory."[358] Of course, the court had gone along with a number of such absurd arguments over the years; O'Connor was simply trying to stop what could be called (ungrammatically) the most absurdest one.

Justice Clarence Thomas wrote his own dissent in the case and wasn't required to salaam the silly *Midkiff* decision, since he wasn't on the court at the time it was made, as O'Connor was. He also assumes that private property is the cornerstone of our system, noting, "The Framers embodied that principle in the Constitution, allowing the government to take property not for 'public necessity,' but instead for 'public use.'" Necessity would allow governments to grab whatever land they felt like, whereas the "use" restriction would allow only land the government itself actually needed, such as for a road or military base. Since the court itself made so many baseless decisions in the past decades, Justice Thomas has to write a sort of third-grader's guide to the Constitution, explaining what the framers meant when they wrote the verb "use" three times in the document, and pointing out that, since Congress was already given the power to do things "necessary and proper"[359] to carry out its responsibilities, the Fifth Amendment's Takings Clause was meant as a *limit on* the government's power, not as a pass to a free lunch. That makes perfect sense (to everyone but a liberal justice) because the entire Bill of Rights is a limit on government power, not a continued list of what the government can get away with if it really wants to. "Still worse," Thomas writes, "it is backwards

---

[357] *Id.* at 429.

[358] *Id.*

[359] U.S. Const. art. I, §8, cl. 18.

to adopt a searching standard of constitutional review for nontraditional property interests, such as welfare benefits, see, *e.g.*, *Goldberg, supra*,[360] while deferring to the legislature's determination as to what constitutes a public use when it exercises the power of eminent domain, and thereby invades individuals' traditional rights in real property."

For once, the public reaction to an asinine Supreme Court decision was fitting. In November 2006, the next major election, "ballot measures to limit eminent domain powers to public uses were approved by large margins in eight states."[361] By that time, thirty-four states had adopted laws to limit the Supreme Court's damage. Of course, liberals did what they could. Wealthy (and appropriately named) developer Howard Rich put together groups in eight states aimed at preserving governmental power to sell out the little guy. In California, opponents of the measure to limit the power of eminent domain used Rich's and other developers' money to outspend the proponents by three-to-one. It was money well spent; they won by just four percentage points.[362] Still, most new laws to block *Kelo* were filled with exceptions stuck in by politicians willing to do the dirty work of wealthy developers. Even in the state where the whole *Kelo* mess arose, the next legislative session ended with no action to curb eminent domain. One report noted that "lawmakers have discussed changing the state's eminent domain laws. The Legislature did pass a law creating an ombudsman to oversee condemnations and help homeowners, but some lawmakers were upset that further measures failed."[363] It's unlikely many were upset, since legislators quickly become backers of using governmental power against its own people. The Democratic speaker of the Connecticut House called it "the most well-run, well-oiled session in 20 years."[364] Oiled, no doubt, by lobbyists' cash.

Oh, and did I mention that after the case meandered all the way to the Supreme Court, the Great Recession that began in 2007 knocked the whole development idea into a cocked hat? All the land that was taken from private owners and given to another private owner under the Takings

---

[360] Goldberg v. Kelly, 397 U.S. 254 (1970). This is the case I took apart in chapter on welfare. What Thomas is saying is, hey, you guys put all these restrictions on government taking away property *it has given* to a citizen by requiring hearings to end welfare payments, et cetera, but you're making it criminally easy to take away property a citizen *has earned.* Makes no sense.

[361] Terry Pristin, "Voters Back Limits on Eminent Domain," *New York Times*, November 15, 2006.

[362] *Id.*

[363] Avi Salzman, "A Session Ends with Little Hoopla," *New York Times,* May 14, 2006.

[364] *Id.*

Clause just sits there now, never having become the shiny new development that city officials claimed would bring new visitors to New London and provide hundreds of jobs. But, like so many other Supreme Court rulings, the damage has been done even if the outcome didn't match what the court expected.

It's unlikely that the recoil to *Kelo* will mean much in the long run. It's too easy to use the public's own tax money against it. Decades ago, the city of Chicago wrecked the lives of thousands through eminent domain in order to build the housing project called Cabrini Green just north of downtown. Even after most of it was demolished years later, a reporter wrote, "Drug dealers form thickets in the lobbies so deep that it resembles a crowded market. The elevators are often out of service, forcing residents into stairwells that addicts have claimed for their own purposes."[365] Decades after the disaster called Cabrini Green, bureaucrats were optimistically pursuing another giant project to replace it, although they had to slide the finish date from 2010 to 2015. They remain sanguine about the outcome and about grabbing the public's cash (years after grabbing its land): "'What drives us is money,' said Sharon Gist Gilliam, the chief executive of the Housing Authority. 'If I could get my hands on a quick $2 billion we could get this done in three or four years.'"[366] Yes, and if the taxpayers could get their money and long-lost property back, they could do a lot with it, too.

---

[365] Susan Saulny, "At Housing Project, Both Fear and Renewal," *New York Times,* March 18, 2007.
[366] *Id.*

THE END OF THE WORLD AS WE KNEW IT *NATIONAL FEDERATION OF INDEPENDENT BUSINESS V. SEBELIUS (2012)*

In the summer of 2012, the Supreme Court allowed the federal government to expand ever onward and outward by allowing the Affordable Care Act ("Obamacare") to become law. Like so many other disastrous decisions by the Court, this one begins with a recitation of how the United States of America should function – and then completely ignores it in extending the powers of the federal government to near infinity. "We do not consider whether the Act embodies sound policies. That judgment is entrusted to the Nation's elected leaders," the opinion by Chief Justice Roberts notes in its first paragraph. That would be a perfectly reasonable statement if the Court had followed it before—say in *Roe v. Wade* or *Mapp v. Ohio,* when the Court changed American society without the slightest input from Congress, but suddenly in 2012, it's the standard against which all decisions must be made. The opinion goes further when it states another truth, that "the Federal Government 'is acknowledged by all to be one of enumerated powers,'" and then quotes the landmark *McCulloch v. Maryland* decision from 1819 that the federal government "can exercise only the powers granted to it." In fact, the powers are very specific, as noted in Article I, Section 8, which the opinion cites. There are eighteen of them, and health care is nowhere in them. Post offices, yes. Armies, sure. Coining money, check. Nope, nothing there that says the federal government is responsible for your nose-wiping. The Chief Justice even notes that the Bill of Rights was added to the Constitution in order to further restrain the power of the federal government, complete with a Tenth Amendment that notes "The powers not delegated to the United States by the Constitution…are reserved to the States respectively, or to the people." Okay, then. Guess that covers it. Obamacare is dead, then, right?

Nope, just fooling! Yet again, the Court uses the once-narrow provisions that Congress can "regulate Commerce with foreign Nations, and among the several States, and with the Indian Tribes," and may "lay and collect Taxes, Duties, Impost and Excises," to mean "Congress can do whatever the hell it wants no matter what the Constitution says."

Clearly the power to "regulate Commerce" meant just that – regulating actual trade between the states, and "laying and collecting taxes" meant, um, laying and collecting taxes. It's doubtful the founders believed the two did not somehow magically add together to mean, "The federal government can ignore the specific enumeration of its powers in Article One, Section Eight that we went to all the trouble of carefully listing here and do what it wants when it wants, thanks to these two statements." If it did, the founders would never have put the Tenth Amendment in the Bill of Rights, nor would they have bothered to enumerate what the federal government was supposed to do. Why limit the powers of the federal government in the Bill of Rights *if no one's going to limit the powers of the federal government?* But in recent years the Supreme Court and Congress have conspired together to decide that, even if the Constitution clearly enumerates the powers of the federal government in a way meant to limit those powers, the Court and Congress will decide to read them in a way that means the federal government has *unlimited* powers.

The Chief Justice goes back to the section of enumerated powers, quoting the final one that Congress can "make all Laws which shall be necessary and proper for carrying into Execution the foregoing powers." Fine. Is national health care one of the "foregoing powers"? No. Then why does that statement give Congress the power to force it on us? Well, Roberts writes, Congress has broad powers dating from *McCulloch v. Maryland,* that early decision that gave the court the power to decide which laws were constitutional. In that decision, Chief Justice Marshall wrote, "Let the end be legitimate, let it be within the scope of the constitution, and all means which are appropriate, which are plainly adapted to that end, which are not prohibited, but consist with the letter and the spirit of the constitution, are constitutional." Okay, let's assume that quote correctly states what the Supreme Court must consider to decide what is constitutional. Where is national health insurance "within the scope of the constitution"? Is it mentioned there? Is any sort of insurance or health care mentioned in the constitution? No? Then wouldn't it be *outside* the scope of the constitution? Note also that Marshall was careful to say that the laws Congress passed must "consist with [be consistent with] the letter and the spirit of the constitution." The letter *and* the spirit. If he had meant the court could make stuff up, he would have written the letter *or* the spirit, but what he said was, it better be written in the constitution (the letter) *and* agree with the spirit of the constitution in order to pass muster. *McCulloch* was written about a case where a state tried to tax a federal bank, hardly a controversial issue in today's world and certainly no relation to a case where the federal government was trying to take over more than a sixth of the entire economy through health care.

The main question is this: we have been told for the past two hundred years that we were the luckiest people in the world because we live in a country that limits the power of its government. Fine. But if so, *where are the limits?* Certainly the Supreme Court has no interest in limiting the power of government, nor does Congress. In the past 60 years, few members of either institution have been interested in defining the limits of federal power, and this is just another example. In his opinion from the Obamacare case, Chief Justice Roberts not only does nothing to stop the federal government's arrogation of yet more power, he actively works to make it easier for them. During the oral arguments in the case, the attorney for the federal government's side was careful to point out that the law's requirement for buying medical insurance did not involve a tax, no sir, wasn't a tax, just a penalty required if you didn't buy the insurance, carefully called a "shared responsibility payment," but later described in the law as a "penalty." The federal district court that first heard the case and the federal appeals court (the Eleventh Circuit) that picked it up from there both agreed that the individual mandate was not a tax. Both rejected the law on those grounds, although their rulings varied somewhat. In fact, Chief Justice Roberts even states that "Congress's decision to label this exaction a 'penalty' rather than a 'tax' is significant because the Affordable Care Act [Obamacare] describes many other exactions it creates as 'taxes.'" But does that mean he's going to declare it unconstitutional, since the federal government has never before been allowed to force people to buy something?

Before he gets to that point, Chief Justice Roberts spends a lot of time talking about how Congress can regulate commerce, but how regulating something that already exists is quite different from forcing someone to do something they hadn't been doing before (buying health insurance). As he writes, "the individual mandate, however, does not regulate existing commercial activity. It instead compels individuals to *become* active in commerce by purchasing a product, on the ground that their failure to do so affects interstate commerce."[367] In fact, he even says, "construing the Commerce Clause to permit Congress to regulate individuals precisely *because* they are doing nothing would open a new and potentially vast domain to congressional authority."[368] Roberts further reaches back to the first case in this book, *Wickard v. Filburn* from 1942, which punished a farmer *not* for selling more wheat than he was allowed under federal law, but for raising *extra* wheat to feed his own animals and family, wheat that was never sold. The Court declared that, even though he had not sold the wheat to anyone, the amount he held back was somehow part of interstate commerce and could be regulated by Congress. To explain the difference between Obamacare's claims and the *Wickard* decision, Roberts says:

> The aggregated decisions of some consumers not to purchase wheat have a substantial effect on the price of wheat, just as decisions not to purchase health insurance have on the price of insurance. Congress can therefore command that those not buying wheat do so, just as it argues here that it may command that those not buying health insurance do so. The farmer in Wickard was at least actively engaged in the production of wheat, and the Government could regulate that activity because of its effect on commerce. The Government's theory here would effectively override that limitation, by establishing that individuals may be regulated under the Commerce Clause whenever enough of them are not doing something the Government would have them do.[369]

---

[367] *National Fed. Of Ind. Bus. v. Sebelius*, 567 U.S. _____, 2012, slip op. at 20.

[368] *Id.*

[369] *National Fed. Of Ind. Bus. v. Sebelius*, 567 U.S. _____, 2012, slip op. at 21-22.

Now notice how many ways Roberts states in his opinion that the federal government has *no right to do* what it wishes with the Affordable Care Act:

1. "Congress addressed the insurance problem by ordering everyone to buy insurance. Under the Government's theory, Congress could address the diet problem by ordering everyone to buy vegetables."[370]

2. "Congress already enjoys vast power to regulate much of what we do. Accepting the government's theory would give Congress the same license to regulate what we do not do, fundamentally changing the relation between the citizen and the Federal Government."[371]

3. "The Framers gave Congress the power to *regulate* commerce, not to *compel* it, and for over 200 years both our decisions and Congress's actions have reflected this understanding. There is no reason to depart from that understanding now."[372]

4. "The individual mandate's regulation of the uninsured as a class is, in fact, particularly divorced from any link to existing commercial activity."[373]

5. "The Commerce Clause is not a general license to regulate an individual from cradle to grave, simply because he will predictably engage in particular transactions."[374]

6. "The individual mandate forces individuals into commerce precisely because they elected to refrain from commercial activity. Such a law cannot be sustained under a clause authorizing Congress to 'regulate Commerce.'"[375]

Certainly, we have finally reached the end of what Congress is allowed to do, right? Roberts has told us in various ways just how the plan to require people to buy health insurance is unconstitutional and outside the range of any decision the Supreme Court has made in the past. So what happens? *He lets it become law anyway.* After all that, the Chief Justice, who earlier strictly noted that the required payment couldn't be a tax because people can't bring suits *before* they pay a tax, now says that the required payment *is* a tax, quoting a 1978 case that "in passing on the constitution-

---

[370] *National Fed. Of Ind. Bus. v. Sebelius*, 567 U.S. _____, 2012, slip op. at 23.

[371] *Id.* at 23-4.

[372] *National Fed. Of Ind. Bus. v. Sebelius*, 567 U.S. _____, 2012, slip op. at 24 (italics in original).

[373] *Id.* at 25.

[374] *Id.* at 26.

[375] *Id.* at 27.

ality of a tax law, we are concerned only with its practical operation, not its definition or the precise form of descriptive words which may be applied to it."[376] So, calling this a "functional approach," and noting that the payment would be collected by the IRS, Roberts calls a tax what the federal government itself never had the temerity to call a tax.

In fact, early in his opinion, Roberts notes that The Anti-Injunction Act, passed by Congress in 1867, made it illegal to bring a lawsuit over payment of taxes if you hadn't already paid the tax. The idea was that a government can't plan on a steady stream of tax revenue if people can refuse to pay a tax and then file suit and tie up things for years, so the law is, pay the damn tax and *then* sue. But notice that Obamacare was sued before any taxes were paid – its payments wouldn't begin until 2014. In order to allow this, the courts had to decide that the mandatory payment for not buying insurance *was not a tax.* If it had been a tax, the suits over the law could not have reached the courts. In fact, Roberts appointed a Friend of the Court (*amicus curiae*) to look into the matter, and stated in the opinion that "*Amicus* contends that the Internal Revenue code treats the penalty as a tax, and that the Anti-Injunction Act therefore bars the suit."[377]

Now, stay with me here:

1. Robert's specially appointed attorney, H. Bartow Farr III (the *amicus curiae*), looked into the situation of whether the individual mandate's penalty was a tax. He decided it was, and because of the Anti-Injunction Act, the suit could not go forward. So, in order to hear the suit, Roberts had to specifically decide that Mr. Farr was far wrong, and that the required payment *was not a tax.*

2. Roberts then declares that Congress has overreached its powers under the Commerce Clause of the constitution, and states it at least six times, as noted above.

3. After deciding the payment was not a tax in order to let the case come before him *and* that the law was an overreach of federal power, Roberts then declares—it's a tax, and Congress has the right to impose it, and because of that, the law can take effect. Here's his quote: "That [the law] seeks to shape decisions about whether to buy health insurance does not mean that it cannot be a valid exercise of the taxing power."[378]

---

[376] *United States v. Sotelo,* 436 U.S. 268, 275 (1978).

[377] *National Fed. Of Ind. Bus. v. Sebelius,* 567 U.S. _____, 2012, slip op. at 12.

[378] *National Fed. Of Ind. Bus. v. Sebelius,* 567 U.S. _____, 2012, slip op. at 31.

See? It's a tax, even if calling it a tax would have meant the suit couldn't be brought in the first place!

And so, after clearly pointing out that Congress does not have the power to do what it wants to do, the Chief Justice hands them the whole kit and kaboodle. The barn doors are open, the horses are out, the fox is in the henhouse, and every other cliché to describe what happens when one snatches defeat from the jaws of victory. Everything else Roberts says to justify his decision to allow the health care takeover is completely overridden by what he already plainly said, that Congress does not have the power to do it, which he said numerous times in various clear ways. In fact, he is finally left to bleat, "It is only because the Commerce Clause does not authorize such a command that it is necessary to reach the taxing power question."[379] Meaning, "I know I said the suit can be heard because the payment is not a tax, and I know I said the law can't be allowed because Congress doesn't have the power under the Constitution, but having done that, I'm now going to call it a tax and let the law stand." What Roberts has done in the opinion is commit nothing less than an impeachable offense, since every justice is required to take an oath swearing to uphold and defend the constitution. He himself clearly states that the requirement to buy health insurance is unconstitutional because Congress does not have the power to call something interstate commerce that involves a person *not* doing something – and then goes ahead and lets the government override the constitution anyway.

What's really odd about the Obamacare debacle is that observers had all been concerned about how justice Anthony Kennedy might vote. He supposedly was the "swing vote" that went back and forth between liberal and conservative. This, liberals claim, is a good thing, although they never seem to urge liberal members of the court to change their votes to more conservative ones. In this case, Kennedy was on the side of conservatives who felt the law overreached – it was Chief Justice Roberts who went over to the Dark Side. The action was so odd that right-wing radio host Michael Savage suggested Roberts's behavior in the case might be related to epilepsy medication he took regularly.

Kennedy, along with Justices Scalia, Thomas and Alito, wrote the dissent, and like most reasoning that makes sense, the objections can be explained quite simply:

---

[379] *National Fed. Of Ind. Bus. v. Sebelius*, 567 U.S. _____, 2012, slip op. at 44.

What is absolutely clear, affirmed by the text of the 1789 Constitution, by the Tenth Amendment ratified in 1791, and by innumerable cases of ours in 220 years since, is that there are structural limits upon federal power—upon what it can prescribe with respect to private conduct, and upon what it can impose on the sovereign States. Whatever may be the conceptual limits upon the Commerce Clause and upon the power to tax and spend, they cannot be such as will enable the Federal Government to regulate all private conduct and to compel the States to function as administrators of federal programs.[380]

Exactly. If there are no limits to the spread of federal power, there is no need for a constitution at all, which is exactly the situation the court has put us in. By continually allowing expansions of the power of the federal government far beyond anything the founders or anyone for a hundred and fifty years after their day would have imagined, our government has been twisted into an overweight, demanding, mandating pile of bureaucracy that exerts so much dead weight upon the nation that its economy is no longer able to support it, hence the stubbornly high unemployment and stubbornly low growth of the GDP and tax revenue in recent years.

In explaining this, the dissenters also reach back to the case that started this book: *Wickard v. Fillburn.* Just as Chief Justice Roberts noted before selling out the nation, the dissenters write, "The striking case of *Wickard v. Fillburn*, which held that the economic activity of growing wheat, even for one's own consumption, affected commerce sufficiently that it could be regulated, has always been regarded as the *ne plus ultra*[381] of expansive Commerce Cause jurisprudence. To go beyond that, and say the *failure* to grow wheat (which is *not* an economic activity, or any activity at all) nonetheless affects commerce and therefore can be federally regulated, is to make mere breathing in and out the basis for federal prescription and extend federal power to virtually all human activity."[382]

The dissent concludes, "The fragmentation of power produced by the structure of our Government is central to liberty, and when we destroy it,

---

[380] *National Fed. Of Ind. Bus. v. Sebelius,* 567 U.S. _____, 2012, slip diss. at 2.

[381] Ultimate, the farthest point.

[382] *National Fed. Of Ind. Bus. v. Sebelius,* 567 U.S. _____, 2012, slip diss. at 3.

we place liberty in peril. Today's decision should have vindicated, should have taught this truth; instead, our judgment today has disregarded it."[383]

Indeed, the *National Federation of Independent Business* case should teach us that the federal government now sees no limits to what it can force citizens to do, and the Supreme Court will do nothing to hold it back. The difference between our current government and that of Czarist Russia or Imperial Japan between the world wars is simply that our government claims to be our friend, not our master. But just as those other two examples, our federal government now believes it can do anything it wants, and apparently we cannot stop it anymore than Russian serfs or Japanese rice farmers could.

---

[383] *Id.* at 65.

WHAT MUST BE DONE

"Power tends to corrupt; absolute power corrupts absolutely." Many people recognize this quote from Lord Acton, but few know it was written to a bishop of the Roman Catholic Church in the nineteenth century at a time when the Church still had near-absolute power over its people. The Church ignored the warning; it's likely the court will too, since few people or organizations have been able to willingly give up power once they have it. Not many Americans understand what a rare thing it was for George Washington to give up power at the end of his second term as president; given his position as the "Father of his country," who would have thrown him out? Certainly no other ruler in the eighteenth century simply handed over all that power and wealth without being forced to.

And so it is with the Supreme Court. It is clear that the framers of the Constitution did not mean for the court to have the power to rule over every law in every state. There are powers allotted to the court in Article III of the Constitution, and the first is over "all Cases, in Law and Equity, arising under this Constitution."[384] That would seem to include everything, except for this: if it includes everything, why does the Constitution then list seven other situations in which cases can be brought before the court? Why not just say the court can do whatever the hell it wants and then stop?

Just as important, why does this all-powerful Supreme Court get shoved to the bottom of the federal pile in Article III? Why didn't Madison

---

[384] U.S. Const. art. III,§ 2.

and the rest simply write, "Article I—the Supreme Court can decide every-thing," and then go home? Why all this talk about what the Congress and the president can do *before* the Supreme Court? Why be so concerned with the limits of congressional and presidential power if the Supreme Court can stop them from doing anything just because it may want to?

And the question I asked earlier in this book: why would the same people who just emerged from the crushing autocracy of British rule, with its king, nobility, and Parliament, want to turn everything over to fewer than half a dozen people who were not elected by the public and who could not be removed from office except for bribery or treason?

If you want to believe the Supreme Court not only has this power but *should* have had this power all along, you then have to ask why it didn't use it all along. Why did it wait more than fifty years after the Fourteenth Amendment was passed to decide, hey, it actually means that our federal Bill of Rights can be used to change any law we want on a state level, and why do it when absolutely every state had a Bill of Rights in its own con-stitution? And if you still believe that, why would the court choose "selec-tive incorporation," meaning that *some* of the Bill of Rights applied to the states, and *some* didn't? Who the hell approved *that?*

What we have lost in this past century is the understanding of what the United States of America was all about. When the Constitution was ham-mered out in Philadelphia, no one expected the laws of Georgia to be the same as those of New Hampshire; all that was needed was enough strength in the federal government to raise money to oversee the defense of and dis-agreements between the states, which had been acting as their own nations (which is what *states* were in those days) and not doing a very good job of it. But total control—why? If the federal government were to run everything, why even bother to keep the states? For bumper stickers travelers could buy and put on their Conestoga wagons? I believe that this country did very well for its first 140 years by allowing states to make most of the deci-sions for themselves,[385] and it wasn't until the twentieth century and the rise of belligerent autocracies that people started thinking, we'd better get on board and start telling *our* citizens what they could and could not do ad infinitum or we'll be defeated. But the truth is now obvious, in the histo-ries of World Wars One and Two, and the collapse of Soviet Communism in

---

[385] The issue of slavery was, I believe, *sui generis*, and didn't have much to do with our form of government. Besides, slavery wasn't just a decision made by those states that practiced it—it required the clear collaboration of those that didn't. When the states that didn't have slavery decided the practice must end, the Civil War began.

1989–91. Dictatorships simply don't work, and we've defeated them every time by being different, not the same. As I've said before, the strength of America is in the opportunity its citizens have to try absolutely everything and then find what works. As much as it seems like a great idea to have a bunch of bureaucrats decide what way to go and put all one's effort in that, just sitting back and letting the creative spirits of individuals take over works better every time, and it works not 5 percent better, but 500 percent better.

So it is with the Supreme Court. *Laissez nous faire.* Leave us be as states and as people to try every kind of law and way of living, and we will see what works best and copy it or not, as we see fit. Some states may legalize abortion and others may damn it to hell. Some will have capital punishment and some will not. Some will have gay marriage and some will have polygamy. Some will have high taxes and some low, but as long as the elections are straight and the cards aren't marked, we'll do just fine.